THE CABBAGETOWN CAFÉ COOKBOOK
by Julie Jordan

The Crossing Press, Freedom, CA 95019

Cover design, cover illustration and text design by Betsy Bayley
Recipe titles by Steve Sierigk
Photographs on back cover and pages 15, 169, 216, and 223
    by Jennifer Kelley
Photographs on pages 125 and 163 by James Cunningham
All remaining photographs by J.E.B. (Joan E. Biren)
Typesetting by Davis Graphics of Lansing, New York

Printed in the U.S.A.
by McNaughton and Gunn of Ann Arbor, Michigan

Library of Congress Cataloging in Publication Data

Jordan, Julie.
   The Cabbagetown Cafe cookbook.

   Includes index.
1. Vegetarian cooking 2. Cabbagetown Cafe
(Ithaca, N.Y.) 3. Cookery--(New York State)
   Ithaca   I. Title
TX837.J55 1986   641.5'636   86-2306
ISBN-0-89594-193-7
ISBN-0-89594-192-9 (pbk.)

for
all the
Cabbages
past, present
and
future

CONTENTS

Introduction

Cabbagetown Café, located in the part of Ithaca, New York, known as Collegetown, was named, appropriately for the early 70s, from a picture on the inside of an album by a rock group called The Band. The storefront which became Cabbagetown had been Elba's, the best pizza place in Ithaca. Elba's moved to a bigger space next door, and several Cornell students, including a group of renovators who lived on a farm near Ithaca, converted the pizza place into a natural foods restaurant. You can still see where the pizza counter was on the dining room floor; but the neon and red and white plastic tablecloth decor was changed to barn boards and white plaster, hanging plants, and handmade wooden tables.

I watched the growth of Cabbagetown as I was only blocks away trying to be a nutrition grad student at Cornell. My heart wasn't in school, in all the sitting and talking. I was a young militant vegetarian and natural foods advocate—I wanted to change the eating habits of the world (by force if necessary). I'd almost finished writing my first cookbook, *Wings of Life*. I gave lectures on vegetarianism, criticized the lab teaching assistants when they used only white flour in the demonstrations, and generally was too energetic and excited to fit into an academic institution.

One day when I was helping to judge the Great Bean Bake-off at Cornell, I felt a hand on my shoulder and turned around to see Ricky Gibson, one of the owners of Cabbagetown Café. "We want you to come cook at our restaurant," he told me.

I thought it over and one morning I just couldn't stay away. I went to Cabbagetown and cooked a pot of minestrone soup. People came to eat my soup and they praised me. I was working with foods I believed in. And I was dashing around a big, well-equipped kitchen actually *doing* something.

I left Cornell and became a Cabbagetown cook. I remember the pure bliss of baking huge batches of bread and laying out smorgasbords at lunch and feeding the crew of renovators when they came in starving and covered with paint from construction jobs. I worked hard and did exactly what I wanted. It's so easy *not* owning a restaurant!

But it was also frustrating. Cabbagetown was started by people of phenomenal good will who wanted to serve the community but who didn't know much about running a restaurant. They hired an assistant cook who asked me how to peel an orange. The waitpeople sat down and talked to their friends instead of waiting on customers. One of the waiters told all the customers that the tarragon flecks in my beautiful crêpes were eggshells.

Craig writing on blackboard

So eventually, like a prima donna, I stormed out and went to California. From California I came back to a brief stint at Cabbagetown. Then I was off to work in the New York vineyards with my friend Steve Tetley from California. Two months later we had just enrolled in grapevine pruning school when the phone rang. "How would the two of you like to *buy* Cabbagetown?"

My immediate instinct was to say "No!" with great determination. But Peter, who ran the vineyard we were working in, told us that we were fools if we didn't take advantage of a chance to operate our own business. He said he'd fire us if we didn't buy Cabbagetown. Steve and I didn't have anything better to do with our lives at that point. It could be an adventure—we'd do it for two years, maximum, then move on. Steve and I had about five hundred dollars between us, but our parents agreed to lend us the money we needed to buy the restaurant.

So there we were, scrubbing and painting the Cabbagetown kitchen white instead of bright orange. I made the restaurant menu out of my wildest dreams and it was drawn up in beautiful calligraphy. On January 6, 1977, about two weeks after we had decided to buy the restaurant, Steve and I reopened the café to an enthusiastic crowd of family, friends, and Ithacans.

I still don't believe how our version of Cabbagetown took off. We were insanely busy on that first night running around and around the counter in the center of the kitchen, totally disorganized, confused and happy. We were rescued by Abby, one of the cooks from the original Cabbagetown, who had stayed on with us. Abby happened to drop in on opening night and single-handedly figured out how to serve lasagne and make omelettes in our chaotic set-up. That was our first night. For about three years we had lines outside the door at every meal.

Steve and I worked overlapping shifts. I worked from 8A.M. to 10P.M. and Steve worked from noon until 2A.M. He always left the restaurant neat and spotless for me and I'd try to cook the best food I could for him. On Steve's "day off" he paid the bills and did the payroll, a job which is done by a half-time accountant now. On my day off I often didn't even get out of bed. It was a crazy way to live.

In the first year I gained about twenty pounds because all I could do to keep up my energy was eat and drink. There was no time or inspiration for exercise or sleep. I got tendonitis of the wrists from kneading too much bread. I became a regular visitor at the chiropractor's office because every week I knocked out my back or my shoulders from running around and lifting and worrying.

Some of Steve's friends came from California to help us. My friends and family in Ithaca also pitched in. (I remember my father saying that helping out at Cabbagetown felt like K.P. duty in the army.) We were lucky to have several wonderful employees who stayed on from the old restaurant as well as the new people we hired and grew to love.

Cabbagetown was my whole world—demanding, intense, rewarding. The hardest trial came when Steve and I split up as a couple but still ran the restaurant together. There were sad and tense days in the kitchen but our employees helped us. Eventually Steve married Teri, a cook and friend from California. They had a gorgeous wedding at Taughannock Falls with a reception at the restaurant. Soon they had a little daughter, Erin, and Steve decided that restaurant life was too unsettled and precarious for a father. I agreed with him totally but this left me with a big decision—we either had to sell the restaurant or I had to buy Steve out.

I bought Steve's half of the restaurant. Without Steve's cool head, I almost managed to run it down to the ground in the first few months. I didn't have any sense of money and went wild with new

Teri, Erin, Steve, and Julie

menu ideas and new staff positions, but I learned and the restaurant pulled through.

Now I'm celebrating my ninth anniversary at Cabbagetown. I've never done anything else for that long. Every single week of those nine years I've contemplated selling the restaurant and never working in a restaurant again in my life. I've complained about rising food costs, moaned about how lonely it was being the boss, and looked for prospective buyers. But I'm still here.

Recently I've come to recognize that everything good in my life in the past nine years has come from Cabbagetown: the people I've met, the money I've used to buy my house, the toughness and strength of character I've developed. I can watch handmade soup tureens crashing to the floor without batting an eyelash. I can listen to my cooks and bookkeepers and best friends telling me that they're leaving town, and I mentally start filling their shifts.

I've developed the feeling that Cabbagetown has its own spirit and its own reason for being. There is no other way it could have survived the health inspectors, the different landlords, construction across the street, and competition around town, not to mention my own lack of business savvy. The restaurant remains so comfortable and warm, fresh and pretty that I feel as if I'm operating in a protected place on the earth. Even though I've spent a lot of time cursing the destiny that drove me to own a restaurant, I'm glad to have done it.

The food at Cabbagetown is almost always wonderful. We use only top-notch natural foods. Through the years the restaurant has attracted some very good cooks. At first I cooked a lot, but my function has evolved toward formalizing a core of recipes and hiring talented human beings and training them. Customers have called Cabbagetown a closet collective. I call it a benevolent monarchy. Whatever it is, it works well most of the time and the Cabbages and I and the customers are happy.

I never thought I'd write another cookbook after *Wings of Life*. My publishers, John and Elaine Gill, were sure I would, and they were right. My first attempt was a Cabbagetown soup cookbook. John and Elaine hinted slyly over carafes of wine and bread and cheese that *all* the food at Cabbagetown was unique and that perhaps I could expand the soup book to a cookbook with all our best recipes in it. I said "No." But here it is.

There is a decided advantage to working with restaurant recipes. They have been made so often that they are streamlined and they are experimented with until they are as delicious as they can possibly be. After a recipe has been batted around in a restaurant kitchen for a few years, you're left with a tattered, penciled-in, almost unreadable card, but it's pure and simple, and often inspired good cooking.

When I've had my weekly crises and episodes of self doubt during the past ten years, I've repeatedly asked myself, "Why am I running this restaurant?" For about four years I did it for Steve. When Steve left, I was without a strong sense of purpose for a while. But around that time I read *Franny and Zooey* by J.D. Salinger and found something that expressed the new kind of inspiration I was feeling. In the story Franny wants to be an actress but is constantly getting discouraged. Her older brother Buddy describes to her an imaginary lady sitting on a porch, whose life is made lovely and special by hearing Franny act on the radio. "Do it for the fat lady," Buddy tells Franny.

All these years a Cornell professor has been coming to Cabbagetown every lunchtime for a bowl of soup, a piece of whole wheat bread, and a dessert (if he's feeling extravagant). We all beam when he walks in, and he is always happy to see us. So now, when I get discouraged or wonder why I'm running Cabbagetown, I say to myself, "Do it for Bart."

Thank you, Bart. Thank you, Cabbages. And thank you, lovely customers.

I hope you readers enjoy our treasured recipes and the anecdotes that go with them. By all means, cook! But don't cook all the time. Go out and eat in restaurants too. We need you.

With love,

Julie waiting on tables

Din and Julie contemplating reseasoning a soup

Hints

Recently I've learned to make homemade **baking powder.** It has all the leavening power of commercial baking powders but none of the metallic aftertaste. To make 1 teaspoon baking powder, mix together 1/2 teaspoon cream of tartar, 1/4 teaspoon baking soda, and 1/4 teaspoon arrowroot or cornstarch. When using any baking powder or soda, rub it between your hands to remove lumps.

Before cooking **beans** for any recipe, we sort them to pick out sticks, stones, and dried-out or dead-looking beans. The most efficient way to do this is to measure the beans and spread them out on a cookie sheet or a large flat baking pan. Starting at the top quickly brush the beans towards the top of the sheet, picking out sticks and stones as you go. Then pour the good beans into a colander and rinse them thoroughly to remove any dirt.

I have a new favorite design for slashing loaves of **bread** before baking. I make 5 short slashes, like the fingers of your hand, radiating out from the bottom of the loaf.

It's easier to beat **butter or cream cheese** if you soften them first. At the restaurant we put them in a metal bowl in a 350°F. oven for just a few minutes. Be careful not to melt butter. At home I put butter or cream cheese in my gas oven, and the heat of the pilot light softens them nicely in about 10 minutes.

I like to eat salads and main dishes with **chopsticks.** With chopsticks I eat more slowly and with more relish.

The Cabbagetown **coffee** blend is one third French roast, two thirds Mocha Java. We serve it with heavy cream, with milk, or black. The staff likes heavy cream.

I think **cole slaw** is an underrated artistic medium. Start with shredded green and red cabbage and add almost anything you like: chopped radishes, scallions, nuts, hard-boiled egg slices. The dressing can be a light vinaigrette or a rich mayonnaise and sour cream mixture.

When you're chopping **fresh green herbs,** use all of the herb that isn't woody. Use parsley stems as well as leaves. Use whole scallions, greens and all. Every tender part of an herb is flavorful and good to eat.

For cutting up **garlic** I recommend my favorite Cabbagetown cooking technique. Smash each peeled garlic clove with the flat side of a Chinese cleaver, then chop it up finely.

Smashing garlic

At the restaurant we buy whole fresh **ginger** and freeze it. Whenever a recipe calls for finely chopped fresh ginger, we break off a piece of the frozen ginger and grate it while it is still frozen. The flavor and texture are excellent.

My favorite **herb tea** blend is spearmint, lemon verbena, rose hips, and licorice. It is especially good brewed with a slice of fresh lemon.

When I'm putting **meals** together at home, I like to serve a first course before the main meal. I like nachos, raw vegetables with dips, anything people can share. For the main course I serve small portions of hot foods such as quiches, enchiladas, pasta. Along with it I serve a big green salad. All wines go well with vegetarian food. I like to wait at least half an hour before serving dessert. Otherwise people just feel glutted and there's no appreciation of a good dessert. Again I serve small portions. I especially like warm fruit desserts (apple crisp for instance) with vanilla ice cream on top.

At Cabbagetown each of us has peeled and chopped at least 1 million **onions,** so we have become quite efficient. First cut off the 2 ends. Next cut the onion in half through the stem end, then peel each half. Chop as usual. Or cut the onion half in crescents. Rest it on its curved side and cut it in slices diagonally out from the center.

When we make **pie crusts or flaky desserts,** we start with cold or frozen butter. Then we grate it into the dough using a hand grater.

Cutting onion crescents

This is very quick, and the pieces are just the right size. I prefer unsalted butter for baking. The taste is better.

All the recipes in this book are lightly salted. If you don't like **salt,** leave it out and salt to taste later.

Soups must be diluted, tasted, and reseasoned after they have been refrigerated or sat awhile.

When **tasting** anything, you want the flavors to stand out clearly. Salt, pepper, and lemon juice will do this. Vinegar brings bean soups to life. Black pepper and thyme sweeten tomato sauces.

At Cabbagetown we don't use an electric mixer. We beat things with **whisks and wooden spoons.** It's quieter and it makes you feel as if you deserve to eat. Din, one of our best waitpeople, used to tell customers they'd have to wait a minute or 2 for the whipped cream on their desserts, then point proudly at us in the kitchen whipping up the cream with a whisk.

Appetizers

Here are the fun foods—nachos, dips, pâtés. We developed our repertoire of appetizers by catering weddings and receptions. We sometimes add bunches of grapes, nicely shaped loaves of homemade bread, and cheeses such as Brie and Jarlsberg to our appetizer table. Along with the appetizers we serve beer, wine, sherry, juices, cider, champagne.

At home I always serve a first course before dinner. One or two appetizers look beautiful on the table and give every meal the feeling of a feast. Guests can come at any time, and we get a chance to mill around and talk before we sit down and focus on the main course. I sometimes serve a big spread of appetizers as the whole meal.

Several of these appetizers might include foods you're not familiar with—tempeh, tahini, dark sesame oil. All the ingredients are available in supermarkets, natural foods stores, or Asian food stores. Once you have them on hand, you'll use them frequently.

Bean and Cheese Nachos

1 cup Craig's Refried Beans (page 23)
1 cup Uncooked Salsa (page 24)
About 24 Tortilla Chips (page 22)
1 cup grated Cheddar or Monterey Jack cheese
1/2 cup sour cream or Guacamole (page 25) (optional)

Nachos are the appetizer we serve most frequently at Cabbagetown. They have a good communal feel.

1. First make the refried beans and salsa, and fry the chips.
2. Heat the refried beans in a small pot or frying pan so the nachos will bake quickly.
3. Spread the beans on an ovenproof serving plate or a 9-inch pie plate. Stick the chips into the beans as artfully as you like. Sprinkle with cheese.
4. Bake in a preheated 350°F. oven for about 15 minutes, until the cheese is melted and bubbly.
5. Remove from the oven. Top with the salsa and the sour cream or guacamole. Serve immediately.

Yield: Serves 4

Tortilla Chips

Corn tortillas
Light vegetable oil

Chips you fry yourself are fresher and more corn-flavored than chips you buy.

1. To make chips, cut the tortillas into sixths using a knife or kitchen scissors.
2. Pour the oil about 1/2 inch deep in a frying pan or wok and place over medium heat until a chip dropped into it sizzles and floats. At that point you are ready to fry.
3. Drop some chips into the oil. Make sure they don't overlap. Use tongs to poke them down into the oil and to flip them over once. Test each chip for doneness by holding it on one tip with the tongs and trying to bend it against the edge of the pan. If it feels stiff and brittle, it's done. Pull each chip out and drain it on a brown paper bag.
4. I like to fry a test batch of chips first to get a feel for how long it will take, and to adjust the flame under the oil so it cooks the chips quickly but doesn't overcook them. The chips are undercooked if they're bendable rather than stiff, and greasy-looking after they cool. You can pop them back in the hot oil and refry them. The chips are overdone if they're browned rather than golden. They will taste bitter. Throw them away and fry your next batch over lower heat or for a shorter time.
5. The chips are fine for nachos if they have cooled down, but if you're serving them with a dip try to serve them hot. Serve them while they're still warm from cooking, or pop them into the oven or toaster oven for 5–10 minutes. Salt to your liking.

Craig's Refried Beans

2 cups uncooked pinto or black beans, sorted for stones and rinsed

6 cups water

2 bay leaves

1 tablespoon ground cumin

1 teaspoon ground coriander

1/2 teaspoon cayenne

1/2 teaspoon black pepper

1/2 teaspoon dried or finely chopped fresh oregano

1/2 teaspoon dried basil or 2 teaspoons finely chopped fresh basil

1/2 teaspoon dried dill weed or 1 tablespoon finely chopped fresh dill

2 1/2 teaspoons salt

3 tablespoons light vegetable oil

1 onion, chopped

1 green pepper, chopped

4 cloves of garlic, finely chopped

1/4 cup butter

1. Measure the beans, water, and bay leaves into a medium-size pot. Bring them to a boil, then reduce the heat and simmer, partially covered, stirring occasionally to keep the beans from sticking. Cook for about 2 hours, or until the beans are very soft.

2. Measure out the spices and salt and mix them together so they are ready to use. In a frying pan, heat the oil. Add the onion, green pepper, and garlic and sauté for about 3 minutes, until limp. Reduce the heat, add the spices and salt, and sauté for 2 minutes more, stirring frequently so nothing sticks and burns.

3. Remove the bay leaves and mash the cooked beans until smooth. Use a potato masher or bean masher or any other mashing device you have. Mash in the vegetable-spice mixture. Mash in the butter.

4. Continue to cook over very low heat for 30 minutes to blend the flavors. Stir often.

5. These beans can be served immediately or stored in the refrigerator for 2–3 days. To reheat, melt a few pats of butter in a frying pan. Add the beans and fry, stirring frequently, until the beans are hot. Serve as a dip for tortilla chips, garnished with a spoonful of sour cream. Or serve refries with nachos, with enchiladas, on tostadas, or as a spicy omelette filling.

QUICK REFRIES
Substitute lentils for the other beans. Decrease water to 5 cups. Lentils cook in 30 minutes.

Yield: 6 cups

Uncooked Salsa

1 quart canned tomatoes or 6 fresh ripe
   tomatoes
2 onions, finely chopped
2 green peppers, finely chopped
2 cloves of garlic, finely chopped
1/4 cup red wine
Juice of 1 lemon
1/2 teaspoon cayenne
1/2 teaspoon dried basil or 2 teaspoons
   finely chopped fresh basil
1/2 teaspoon dried or finely chopped fresh
   oregano
1/2 teaspoon salt

Craig invented this fresh and zippy uncooked salsa after new cooks managed to burn the cooked salsa an alarming number of times.

1. Pour canned tomatoes through a strainer or a colander mounted in a bowl to drain off some juice. You will need about 2 1/2 cups of mostly drained tomatoes to make a thick salsa. (Save the tomato juice to use in soup or in your refried beans.)
2. Finely chop the drained tomatoes or squeeze them with your hands to make small pieces. If you are using fresh tomatoes, chop them up finely.
3. Mix all the other ingredients into the chopped tomatoes.
4. Taste and adjust the seasonings.
5. Let the salsa stand for about 30 minutes so the flavors can blend, then serve it immediately for maximum fresh taste. This salsa will keep for 2–3 days in the refrigerator.

Yield: 4 cups

Guacamole

1 ripe avocado
2 tablespoons sour cream
1/4 small onion or 2 scallions, finely
   chopped
Pinch salt
Squeeze of fresh lemon juice
1 clove of garlic, finely chopped (optional)
1/4 teaspoon ground cumin (optional)

The secret to making good guacamole is to start with good avocados. I suggest buying the ones from California. I also suggest buying avocados that are well on their way to being ripe, since you can't tell whether a rock-hard avocado will ripen or just rot. A nicely ripening avocado will be unbruised, and when you squeeze it gently, it will hold the impression of your fingers. To finish ripening the avocado, leave it at room temperature. When it feels firm but soft all the way through it's ready. If it feels hard, wait.

1. The easiest way to peel an avocado is to cut it into wedges, then pull the skin off each wedge. Put the peeled avocado into a medium-size bowl and mash it with a fork.
2. With the fork, beat in the sour cream until the mixture is fluffy. Mix in the onion or scallions, salt, and lemon juice. Taste. Add more salt or lemon juice if the guacamole is lacking in flavor. If you started with a good avocado, this is all you need. If the avocado you started with was slightly bland, add the garlic and cumin.
3. Serve right away on top of nachos, as a dip for tortilla chips or carrot sticks, on hot buttered bread for guacamole sandwiches, or as an omelette filling. If you must store the guacamole, don't keep it for more than an hour or it will turn brown and develop an off flavor. Sprinkle it with lemon juice, cover it with waxed paper so no air can get to it, and keep it in the refrigerator.

Yield: About 1 cup

The World's Best Garlic Bread

1 cup butter, at room temperature
16 cloves (2 bulbs) of garlic, finely chopped
1/4 cup finely chopped fresh parsley
1/2 cup freshly grated Parmesan cheese
1 teaspoon dried or finely chopped fresh
  oregano
1/4 teaspoon salt
1 cup drained canned tomatoes or 2 fresh
  tomatoes, chopped into small pieces
8–12 slices whole wheat bread (Homemade
  bread is best.)

Sixteen cloves seems like a lot of garlic, but the garlic blends with the butter and tomatoes to give you something very rich.

1. In a medium-size mixing bowl, beat the softened butter until it's smooth.
2. Mix in the garlic, parsley, Parmesan, oregano, and salt.
3. Mix in the tomatoes, but don't mix until they are smooth. You want the tomatoes to be in irregular lumps.
4. Spread the mixture thickly on the slices of bread.
5. Lay out flat on baking trays and bake in a preheated 350°F. oven for about 25–30 minutes, until the butter is melted in and the slices look hot and luscious.
6. Serve with the first course, or with a big salad, or with pasta.

Yield: Serves 8–12

Onion Pakoras

6 onions, cut in crescents
Juice of 2 lemons
1 tablespoon salt (Yes, I mean a
    tablespoon.)
1 teaspoon cayenne
1 tablespoon ground cumin
1 tablespoon cumin seeds
2 cups chick-pea flour (also called besan;
    available in Asian and Middle Eastern
    food stores)
Light vegetable oil for frying

These spicy fritters from India always steal the show.

1. Mix together the onions, lemon juice, salt, and spices. In India the mixing is done vigorously with the hands. Squeeze the spices into the onions. Let sit for 30–60 minutes. The onions will throw off juice, which will be part of the batter with the chick-pea flour later.
2. After the sitting time, mix in the chick-pea flour.
3. In a medium-size frying pan, heat oil about 1/2 inch deep until a tiny bit of the batter dropped in it sizzles. Pull out small handfuls of the onion mixture and drop them in the oil. Fry each pakora until browned and crisp, turning once. Drain on paper towels or on a brown paper bag.
4. Serve hot. These are best absolutely fresh, but they heat up nicely in the oven.

CRISP ONION PAKORAS
Add 2–3 tablespoons rice flour to the recipe to make a crisper pakora.

CABBAGE OR SPINACH PAKORAS
Replace 2 of the onions with 2 cups very finely cut cabbage or spinach.

ZUCCHINI PAKORAS
Replace 2 of the onions with 2 cups grated zucchini.

Yield: 32 pakoras. Serves 8–12

Marinated Brussels Sprouts

1 pound brussels sprouts
1 cup Tarragon Vinaigrette Dressing
  (page 71)
1 teaspoon fennel seeds

For a hedonistic start to a meal, try serving these with Brie, crackers, and sherry or white wine.

1. Prepare the brussels sprouts by rinsing them and trimming off the browned tips of the stems and any yellowed leaves. Steam or blanch them for 8–12 minutes, until they are barely tender when pierced with a fork. Pour through a colander to drain off the water.
2. Prepare the dressing. Mix in the fennel seeds. Pour into a medium-size pot and simmer for 1–2 minutes to blend the flavors. Add the cooked sprouts and toss together. Remove from the heat and allow to cool, tossing occasionally so all the sprouts are covered with dressing.
3. Serve at room temperature. You can store them in the refrigerator and remove 30 minutes before serving so they can warm up. I like putting out fondue forks so people can spear the sprouts.

MARINATED MUSHROOMS
Rinse 1 pound of mushrooms thoroughly and trim off any browned spots. Drop the mushrooms into a pot of boiling water and boil for 5 minutes. Pour through a colander to drain the water. Then proceed as with brussels sprouts.

Yield: Serves 4–6

Creamy Lemon Dip

1 egg
1/2 teaspoon salt
1 tablespoon red wine vinegar
2 cloves of garlic
1 cup light vegetable oil
Juice of 1 lemon
1 tablespoon prepared French mustard
1/2 teaspoon black pepper
1 tablespoon dried green herbs or 1/2–1
   cup lightly packed fresh green herbs
   (Some fresh coriander leaves are
   especially good.)

I frequently make this dip at home. It's a fancy mayonnaise, and you can add different flavorings to suit your moods.

1. If you're using a whisk, finely chop the garlic and the fresh green herbs. If you're using a blender, you can add them whole and the blender will chop them.
2. Whisk or blend the egg with the salt, vinegar, and garlic until creamy.
3. Whisking or blending constantly, add about 1/2–2/3 cup of the oil in a slow trickle. At some point the mayonnaise will take and become much thicker.
4. After it thickens, continue beating in the remaining oil alternately with the lemon juice.
5. Whisk or blend in the mustard, pepper, and herbs.
6. Taste on a vegetable stick and adjust the seasonings if needed.
7. Serve as a dip with fresh carrot sticks, mushrooms, and zucchini, or with steamed broccoli and cauliflower.

CREAMY CUMIN DIP
Blend or whisk in 1 teaspoon of ground cumin.

CREAMY CAPER DIP
Omit the salt and blend or whisk in 1 tablespoon of capers.

Yield: 2 cups

Garden Cream Cheese Dip

8 ounces cream cheese, at room
    temperature
3-inch piece of carrot, peeled, grated, and
    chopped
6-inch piece of celery stalk, finely chopped
Wedge of green pepper, finely chopped
1 scallion, finely chopped
A few sprigs of parsley, finely chopped
2 teaspoons caraway seeds, toasted in a
    frying pan
Freshly ground black pepper

This cream cheese dip, flecked with tiny pieces of colorful vegetables, is a major hit at our catering jobs. We also served this on buttered toast or hot bagels at the restaurant when we were doing breakfast.

1. In a medium-size mixing bowl, beat the cream cheese with a fork.
2. Beat in all the other ingredients and continue beating until the mixture is smooth.
3. Allow the dip to sit for at least 15 minutes before serving so the flavors can mingle. Or refrigerate until you are ready to use it.
4. Serve as a dip with raw vegetables, especially raw cauliflower, radishes, and carrot sticks.

Yield: Serves 4

Cream Cheese and Fresh Herb Dip

8 ounces cream cheese, at room
  temperature
1/4 cup chopped fresh parsley
2 tablespoons finely chopped fresh chives
  or scallions
2 tablespoons finely chopped fresh dill
1/4 cup heavy cream
Freshly ground black pepper

Make this in the summer with fresh herbs.

1. In a medium-size mixing bowl, beat the
cream cheese with a fork.
2. Beat in the herbs.
3. Beat in the cream until the mixture is
smooth and fluffy. Grind in the black pepper.
4. Taste and adjust the seasonings if needed.
5. Serve as a dip with raw vegetables,
especially cucumbers. Or spread it on crackers
and top with a slice of ripe, ripe red tomato.

Yield: Serves 4

Cream Cheese and Black Olive Dip

8 ounces cream cheese, at room
   temperature
1/2 cup chopped black olives
2 tablespoons finely chopped fresh chives
   or scallions
1/4 cup heavy cream

The better the olives, the better the spread. If you have the patience, cut your favorite olives off the pits and chop them. (I think oil-cured olives are better tasting than brine-cured.)

1. In a medium-size mixing bowl, beat the cream cheese with a fork.
2. Beat in the olives and the chives or scallions.
3. Beat in the cream until the mixture is smooth and fluffy.
4. Allow the dip to sit for at least 15 minutes before serving so the flavors can mingle, or refrigerate until you're ready to use it.
5. Serve as a dip with raw vegetables or spread it on crackers.

Yield: Serves 4

Steve's Tofu Salad

2 cups crumbled tofu (1 pound)
2 1/2 tablespoons tamari or soy sauce
1 tablespoon red wine vinegar
2 tablespoons dark sesame oil
1/2 cup tahini
2 cloves of garlic, finely chopped
1 teaspoon turmeric
1/2 teaspoon ground cumin
Pinch cayenne
1 carrot, grated
1 celery stalk, finely chopped
1/2 green pepper, finely chopped
1 small onion, finely chopped (optional)

This salad has nice colors and a smooth texture. Many fans say it is like a vegetarian chopped liver.

1. In a medium-size mixing bowl, mash the tofu with a fork.
2. As you add the other ingredients, continue to cream the mixture with a fork until it's smooth and creamy, and has a light consistency.
3. Taste and reseason if needed.
4. Chill before serving. Decorate with finely grated carrots, and serve as a spread on crackers.

Yield: 3 cups

Jill's Tempeh Salad

1/2 pound tempeh
1 tablespoon tamari or soy sauce
1/2 small red onion, finely chopped
1 celery stalk, finely chopped
About 3 tablespoons mayonnaise or
Rugged Garlic Dressing (page 68)
1/4 teaspoon salt
Pinch cayenne

This is a gentle and pleasing way to introduce yourself and other people to tempeh. Tempeh is a traditional Indonesian fermented soybean food, which is now gaining popularity with vegetarians because of its nutritional value and rich savory taste. You can buy it fresh or frozen at natural foods stores. I've found that tempeh is much richer and more succulent if you boil it with a little tamari or soy sauce before you use it, so all the tempeh recipes in this book start with that step.

1. Put the tempeh in boiling water to which you've added 1 tablespoon tamari or soy sauce. Return to a boil, then boil gently for 20 minutes. Pour through a colander to drain off the water.
2. In a medium-size bowl, mash the tempeh with a fork. Mix in the onion and celery ("plus anything crunchy your Mom used to put in tuna salad," says Jill).
3. Mix in enough mayonnaise or Rugged Garlic Dressing to make the salad moist but not mushy. Mix in the salt and cayenne.
4. Taste for salt. Jill suggests you might also want to add 1 clove of garlic, mashed.
5. Chill before serving. Serve as a spread on crackers or as a dip for celery, carrot, and cucumber sticks, or tomato wedges. Or serve it on hot buttered toast with horseradish and tomato slices for tempeh salad sandwiches.

Yield: 3 cups

Hummus

1 cup uncooked chick-peas, sorted for
stones and rinsed (2 cups cooked)
5 cups water
2 bay leaves
2 cloves of garlic, finely chopped
1/2 teaspoon salt
3/4 cup tahini
Juice of 1 lemon
About 1/4 cup chick-pea cooking liquid or
water
1/2 cup finely chopped fresh parsley
2 tablespoons finely chopped fresh chives
or scallions
1 celery stalk, finely chopped (optional)

An Arabic customer said this was the best
hummus he'd tasted in the United States.

1. Measure the chick-peas, water, and bay
leaves into a medium-size pot. Bring to a boil,
then reduce the heat and simmer, partially
covered, stirring occasionally to keep the chick-
peas from sticking. Cook for 2–3 hours, or
until the chick-peas are very tender.
2. In a medium-size bowl, mix the garlic, salt,
and tahini with a wooden spoon. Mix in the
lemon juice a little at a time, alternating with
the chick-pea cooking liquid. Continue adding
liquid until the mixture whips up and lightens
in color. Even if the mixture appears to
curdle, just keep adding liquid and beating. It
will come together. Getting the whipped
consistency is crucial for the final consistency
of the hummus.
3. Grind the chick-peas through a meat
grinder, grain mill, or food processor. A
blender will not work.
4. Stir the chick-peas into the tahini mixture.
Add the parsley, chives or scallions, and
celery. If the mixture is too thick, stir in more
chick-pea liquid until it's fluffy.
5. Taste. You might want to add more salt,
lemon juice, or parsley.
6. Serve as a dip with carrot, celery, and
cucumber sticks, radishes, whole scallions, or
steamed broccoli. Serve as a spread on
crackers. Or serve on hot buttered bread or in
pita bread for hummus sandwiches.

Yield: 3 cups

Nut and Mushroom Pâté

1/2 cup mixed nuts and seeds
2 tablespoons olive oil
1 onion, very finely chopped
1 pound mushrooms, very finely chopped
1/2 cup crumbled tofu
1/4 cup olive oil
1/4 cup tahini
2 tablespoons tamari or soy sauce
Juice of 1/2 lemon
1 clove of garlic, finely chopped
1/2 teaspoon dried or finely chopped fresh oregano
1/2 teaspoon dried or finely chopped fresh tarragon
1/2 teaspoon mustard powder

The idea for this pâté came from Bloodroot Restaurant in Bridgeport, Connecticut. We've changed their recipe a little. Bloodroot has published two very good cookbooks called *The Political Palate.*

1. Toast the nuts and seeds in a toaster oven or in a frying pan until lightly browned.
2. Heat 2 tablespoons oil in a frying pan and add the onion and mushrooms. Fry until the mixture is dark brown and dry. Do not burn.
3. In a blender, combine the tofu, 1/4 cup oil, the tahini, tamari, lemon juice, and seasonings and blend until smooth. Add the toasted nuts and seeds, and blend until almost smooth. (A little crunchy texture is nice here.)
4. Remove the blended mixture to a bowl. Stir in the mushrooms and onion.
5. Allow to cool, then taste and adjust seasonings as needed. I sometimes like to add a little salt.
6. Serve as a dip for carrot and celery sticks and steamed broccoli or cauliflower. Or use it as a spread on crackers.

Yield: 2 cups

Breads

When Cabbagetown first opened, my friend Patti and I used to walk down there almost every day to get soup and corn bread for lunch. That corn bread was the best you could imagine—hot from the oven and steamy, with lots of butter.

A few months later, when I started working at Cabbagetown, I found out that they purchased their whole wheat bread. That seemed all wrong to me. I felt that bread baking was crucial to the rhythm, to the warmth and the smells of the restaurant.

When Steve and I bought the restaurant, I started making all the whole wheat bread, ten loaves a day, six days a week. After six months, the strain of so much kneading gave me tendonitis of the wrists, and I had to wear ace bandages and stop making bread. However, making bread had caught on with the other cooks by then, and it became the highest honor in the Cabbagetown cooking hierarchy. Making bread became the real heart of Cabbagetown.

Cabbagetown bread is always made from whole grains with honey or molasses as sweeteners. It is all made by hand. There are a few recipes but no definite rules; each baker simply puts his or her heart and soul into it. The bread is never the same from day to day, but it is always wonderful.

On Sundays, in the middle of the bustling Sunday brunch kitchen, Matthew started making very light round loaves of bread with seeds on top. Matthew is one of the few people who changed my tastes in food. He won me over from the dense, almost cake-like breads I'd preferred to lighter, crusty loaves. The method I give in this chapter is largely his.

Cabbagetown Corn Bread

1 1/4 cups cornmeal
3/4 cup whole wheat pastry flour
1/4 cup dried milk powder
1 teaspoon salt
2 teaspoons baking powder
1 egg
1/4 cup honey
1 cup milk
3 tablespoons light vegetable oil

This corn bread is famous throughout Ithaca, and in many other places as well. For 7 years I tried to scale down our restaurant recipe to a home-size version. This is very close. Use the freshest cornmeal you can get and be sure to use whole wheat *pastry* flour.

1. In a medium-size bowl, mix together the cornmeal, flour, milk powder, and salt. Mix in the baking powder, rubbing it between your hands as you add it so there are no lumps.
2. Make a well in the center of the dry ingredients, and in it beat the egg lightly. Mix the honey, milk, and oil into the egg.
3. Mix the wet ingredients into the dry, and beat thoroughly so the batter is smooth and there are no lumps.
4. Pour the batter into a well-buttered 9-inch pie pan. Bake in a preheated 350°F. oven for 25–30 minutes, until the corn bread is firm and lightly browned. Serve warm from the oven with plenty of butter.
5. Often variations in the kinds of cornmeal and pastry flour you use will cause variation in the final texture of the corn bread. If you make this recipe once and the corn bread is dry, try adding more milk to the batter. If the corn bread is too wet and dense, add more cornmeal.

Yield: One 9-inch corn bread

Cabbagetown Whole Wheat Bread

3 cups hot water
1/3 cup honey
2 tablespoons active dry yeast
4 cups whole wheat bread flour
3 tablespoons oil
2 1/2 teaspoons salt
About 2 cups whole wheat bread flour
Cornmeal

This is our basic bread recipe with complete instructions and a few good variations. The secret to getting a good-textured bread is to work with a fairly wet dough and to give it plenty of time to rise.

1. Measure the water into a bread bowl. In it dissolve the honey, stirring with a wooden spoon.
2. Drop the yeast into the water while it is still warm. (The ideal water temperature is 110°F. You can drip it on the underside of your wrist and the water will feel the same as your body temperature.) Leave the water-yeast mixture for about 5 minutes, while the yeast dissolves and begins to foam.
3. Gradually add 4 cups whole wheat bread flour, stirring until the mixture is smooth.
4. Leave this "sponge" to rise in a warm spot for 1–2 hours, stirring it down once or twice as it gets high.
5. Pour in the oil around the edges of the bowl. Stir it in, along with the salt.
6. Gradually add more whole wheat flour, stirring in 1 direction all the time to work up gluten most effectively. Continue adding flour only until the dough holds together. It will still be fairly wet. The amount of flour you use will vary depending on the gluten content of the flour.
7. Turn the dough onto a lightly floured counter and knead for 5 minutes. Be light-handed. Resist the temptation to knead in too much flour. The dough should continue to be sticky and hard to work with, since a slightly wet dough is best for gluten formation. Dust

the counter with flour only as needed. You've kneaded enough when you can poke the dough with your thumb and the dough springs back.

8. Lightly oil the bread bowl and return the dough to it.

9. Allow the dough to rise in a warm spot for 1–2 hours, or until it is more than double in bulk. Punch it down.

10. Divide the dough into 2 or 3 portions, depending on the number of loaves you want. Knead each portion of dough until it holds together in a smooth ball. Leave the balls on a lightly floured counter to rise for 1–2 hours, or until they're more than double in bulk.

11. Punch down. Shape each ball into a loaf and arrange on cookie sheets sprinkled with cornmeal.

12. Let the loaves rise in a warm spot for about 45 minutes, or until double in bulk.

13. Slash with a serrated knife.

14. Place the loaves in a preheated 350°F. oven. Bake until the loaves are firm and golden brown, and sound hollow when tapped on the bottom. Large loaves bake in about 60 minutes. Smaller loaves bake in 40–50 minutes.

15. Remove from the pans and allow to cool on cooling racks.

GLAZED WHOLE WHEAT BREAD
Right before you bake the loaves, beat an egg with a fork. Brush it on the tops of the loaves with a pastry brush. Slash with a serrated knife. Sprinkle with poppy or sesame seeds or a mixture of both. Bake as usual.

OATMEAL BREAD
Cook 1 cup rolled oats in 1 cup water until soft, about 1–2 minutes. Melt in 1/2 cup butter. Add this at step 5 instead of the oil.

POPPY SEED BREAD
Add 1/3 cup of poppy seeds at step 5.

CRUNCHY MILLET BREAD
Add 1/2 cup uncooked millet at step 5.

MATTHEW'S BREAD
Add 1/4 cup sesame seeds or caraway seeds at step 5. Roll some finely chopped fresh parsley or dill into the loaves as you shape them.

ONION BREAD
Sauté 2 finely chopped onions very lightly in 2 tablespoons butter. Work the onions into the dough as you shape the loaves.

SUBTLE SOURDOUGH
Make the regular whole wheat bread recipe, but instead of leaving the sponge for 1–2 hours, leave it to rise and ferment overnight. Then continue as usual. This will give your bread a subtle and pleasing sourdough taste.

Yield: 2 or 3 loaves

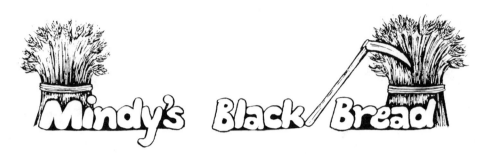

Mindy's Black Bread

3 cups hot water (or combination hot
    water and hot coffee)
1/4 cup honey
1/4 cup molasses
2 tablespoons active dry yeast
4 cups whole wheat bread flour
1/4 cup butter
2 tablespoons fennel seeds
2 teaspoons salt
1/2 cup carob powder or Pero or Postum
    powder
About 2 cups whole wheat bread flour
Cornmeal
1 egg
2 teaspoons caraway seeds

This dark black bread has a taste that brought customers back for years of Thursdays, Mindy's bread day. It's especially good with cream cheese spreads.

1. Measure the water (or water and coffee) into a bread bowl. In it dissolve the honey and molasses, stirring with a wooden spoon.
2. Drop the yeast into the water while it is still warm. Leave the water-yeast mixture for about 5 minutes, while the yeast dissolves and begins to foam.
3. Gradually add 4 cups whole wheat bread flour, stirring until the mixture is smooth.
4. Leave this sponge to rise in a warm spot for 1–2 hours, stirring it down once or twice as it gets high.
5. Melt the butter in a small saucepan. Add the fennel seeds and sauté for 1–2 minutes to enhance their flavor. Pour this mixture into the sponge. Stir it in, along with the salt and carob powder.
6. Gradually add more whole wheat flour, stirring in 1 direction to work up the gluten most effectively. Continue adding flour until the dough holds together but is still fairly wet.
7. Turn the dough onto a lightly floured counter and knead for 5 minutes. Dust the counter with flour only as needed. You've kneaded enough when you can poke the dough with your thumb and the dough springs back.
8. Lightly oil the bread bowl and return the dough to it.
9. Allow the dough to rise in a warm spot for 1–2 hours, or until it is more than double in

bulk. Punch it down.

10. Divide the dough into 2 or 3 portions, depending on the number of loaves you want. Knead each portion of dough until it holds together in a smooth ball. Leave the balls on a lightly floured counter to rise for 1–2 hours, or until they're more than double in bulk.

11. Punch down. Shape each ball into a loaf and arrange on cookie sheets sprinkled with cornmeal.

12. Let the loaves rise in a warm spot for about 45 minutes, or until double in bulk.

13. To glaze the loaves, beat 1 egg with a fork. Brush it on the tops of the loaves with a pastry brush. Slash with a serrated knife. Sprinkle with caraway seeds.

14. Place the loaves in a preheated 350°F. oven, and bake until the loaves are firm and sound hollow when tapped on the bottom, 45–60 minutes depending on the size of your loaves. If you have any beaten egg left over, brush the loaves once more while they bake.

15. Remove from the pans and allow to cool on cooling racks.

Yield: 2 or 3 loaves

Craig's Sourdough Bread

YEAST SPONGE

2 cups hot water
1/4 cup honey
1 tablespoon active dry yeast
About 2 1/2 cups whole wheat bread flour

SOURDOUGH SPONGE

1 cup hot water
1/4 cup honey
2 cups Sourdough Starter (page 46)
About 1 1/2 cups whole wheat bread flour

FINISHING THE BREAD

3 tablespoons oil
2 1/2 teaspoons salt
About 2 cups whole wheat bread flour
Cornmeal

Sourdough breads take longer to make than other yeast breads, but the added zippy flavor is worth it. I recommend starting sourdough breads early in the morning to have them done for dinner-time. Craig likes to make 2 sponges—a yeast sponge and a sourdough sponge—then mix them together. The yeast makes the bread light and crusty, and the sourdough adds a distinctive flavor.

1. To make the yeast sponge, measure 2 cups hot water into a bread bowl. In it dissolve 2 tablespoons honey, stirring with a wooden spoon. While the water is still warm, drop in 1 tablespoon yeast. When the mixture foams, stir in about 2 1/2 cups flour, enough to make a loose sponge.
2. To make the sourdough sponge, measure 1 cup hot water into a medium-size or large bowl. In it dissolve 2 tablespoons honey, stirring with a wooden spoon. While the mixture is still hot, mix in the sourdough starter. Mix in about 1 1/2 cups flour, enough to make a loose sponge.
3. Set the 2 sponges in a warm spot to rise for 2–4 hours, depending on your schedule. Stir down once or twice as the sponges get high.
4. Combine the 2 sponges in the bread bowl. Stir in the oil and salt. Turn onto a lightly floured counter and knead for 5 minutes, adding just enough flour to hold the dough together. Be careful not to add too much flour; the dough should be slightly wet.
5. Lightly oil the bread bowl and return the dough to the bowl. Leave it to rise in a warm

spot for 2–3 hours, or until it is more than double in bulk. Punch it down.

6. Divide the dough into 2 or 3 portions, depending on the number of loaves you want. Knead each portion of dough until it holds together in a smooth ball. Leave the loaves on a lightly floured counter to rise for 2 hours.

7. Punch down. Shape each ball into a loaf and arrange on cookie sheets sprinkled with cornmeal.

8. Let the loaves rise in a warm spot for about 2 hours, or until double in bulk.

9. Right before baking, slash the loaves with a serrated knife, and spray or rub them with water. The water will help form a crusty loaf.

10. Bake in a preheated 350°F. oven for 20 minutes. Spray or rub the loaves with water again. Turn the oven down to 325°F. and continue baking for about 20–30 minutes, until the loaves are done. Sourdough breads brown more quickly than regular breads, so be sure you feel them when testing them for doneness. The loaves are done when they are firm and sound hollow when tapped on the bottom.

11. To get the maximum crust remove the loaves from the cookie sheets and place on cooling racks. Return the loaves on the cooling racks to the oven for about 5 minutes. Then remove from the oven and continue cooling as usual.

Yield: 2 or 3 loaves

Sourdough Starter

1 tablespoon active dry yeast
3 cups warm water
3 cups whole wheat bread flour or rye
  flour

If you'd like to make sourdough bread and don't have a starter, I recommend finding friends who have one and asking them to share it or buying a commercial dried sourdough starter. You can also make your own, although it will be a bit harsher than a commercial one. Here's a recipe for making a sourdough starter, and instructions for caring for starters.

1. Mix together the ingredients in a non-metal bowl.
2. Cover the bowl with a clean towel. Leave the mixture for 3 days at room temperature until it is bubbly and sour. The microorganisms in homemade starters are more random than those in commercial starters, but you can tell a lot about the taste your bread will have from the smell of your starter at this point.
3. Transfer the starter to a covered crock or to a loosely covered glass jar. (A bail-wire canning jar is good.) If you use the culture every few days, you can leave it out at room temperature and the culture will be very lively. If you use it less often, keep it in the refrigerator. It's good to keep 3–4 cups of starter in the jar so you use about half of your culture each time you make bread.
4. Whenever you make sourdough bread, stir up the starter and use what you need of it. Build the starter back to its original volume by mixing in equal parts of whole wheat bread flour and warm water. This gives the microorganisms new food so they can keep growing.

5. If you haven't used the starter in a long time—say about a month—pour it out of its jar into a bowl, feed it with a little flour and water, and leave it out at room temperature to give the microorganisms a boost. Then clean the jar and return the starter. (Clean the jar occasionally even if you use the starter regularly.) If you take care of it—feed it, clean its house, and exercise it—your sourdough starter will stay fresh and peppy for years.

Yield: 3–4 cups

Julie shaping loaves of bread

Sesame Dinner Rolls

1 1/2 cups hot water
1/4 cup honey
1 tablespoon active dry yeast
2 teaspoons dried dill weed or 2
   tablespoons finely chopped fresh dill
2 cups whole wheat bread flour
6 tablespoons butter
1/4 cup sesame seeds
1 teaspoon salt
About 1 cup whole wheat bread flour

These buttery little morsels are quicker to make than loaves of bread—about 2 hours from start to finish—and they don't require kneading. So they're ideal when you want fast uncomplicated bread.

1. Measure the water into a medium-size or large bowl. In it dissolve the honey, stirring with a wooden spoon.
2. Drop the yeast into the water while it is still warm. Leave the mixture for about 5 minutes, while the yeast dissolves and foams.
3. Stir in the dill, then 2 cups bread flour.
4. Leave this sponge to rise in a warm spot for about 30 minutes.
5. In a small frying pan, melt the butter and add the sesame seeds. Sauté until lightly browned. Mix into the sponge, along with the salt.
6. Stir in about 1 cup whole wheat bread flour. You want a fairly wet and sticky dough.
7. Allow to rise in a warm spot for 20–30 minutes.
8. Butter 10 cups in a standard muffin tin.
9. Stir down the dough. To shape rolls, pull off small balls of dough and roll lightly into balls with your hands. Fit 3 balls into each muffin cup. The cup will be about 3/4 full.
10. Allow the rolls to rise in a warm spot for 15–30 minutes, until they just rise over the edges of the muffin cups.
11. Bake in a preheated 350°F. oven for about 30 minutes, or until the rolls are lightly browned. Remove immediately from the pans and serve warm.

Yield: 10 rolls

Midori's Ricotta Popovers

15–16 ounces ricotta cheese (about 2 cups)
1 egg
1 cup whole wheat pastry flour
1/4 teaspoon salt

These are fast, easy to make, and yummy. They must be eaten right away.

1. Mix together all the ingredients. You can either bake the popovers at this time or store the dough in the refrigerator until you are ready to use it.
2. With well-floured hands, shape the dough into balls the size of golf balls. Arrange on a buttered cookie sheet, leaving each ball enough room to puff up slightly.
3. Bake in a preheated 350°F. oven for about 40 minutes, or until the popovers are lightly browned and starting to get crusty. Serve immediately with butter.

Yield: 12 popovers

Jude's Cheese Herb Biscuits

2 cups whole wheat pastry flour
2 teaspoons baking powder
1/2 teaspoon salt
1/2 teaspoon dried basil or 1 teaspoon finely chopped fresh basil
1/2 teaspoon dried or finely chopped fresh thyme
1/4 cup cold butter
1/2 pound Cheddar or Swiss cheese, grated (2 cups)
3/4 cup milk or buttermilk

These biscuits are quick to make and very flavorful— good to serve with hot soup.

1. In a medium-size bowl, mix together the dry ingredients.
2. Grate in the butter. Toss it in with a fork. Then toss in the grated cheese. Mix in the milk or buttermilk.
3. Knead the dough in the bowl until it holds together. If it doesn't hold together, add a little more liquid. Form into 8–10 balls, flatten each ball a bit, and place on an ungreased cookie sheet.
4. Bake in a preheated 350°F. oven for about 25 minutes, or until lightly browned. Serve at once while still hot.

Yield: 8–10 biscuits

Salads

Our house salad in the winter is a base of fresh spinach and romaine lettuce with grated red and white cabbage, grated carrots, and sprouts. In the summer we use every green under the sun. We've all spent countless hours washing lettuce, washing and destemming spinach, tearing lettuce, grating carrots (and our knuckles), and mixing it all together. We tear the lettuce rather than cut it with a knife because the flavor is better and the edges don't brown. I'm a tyrant about tearing lettuce correctly. You must snap each leaf rather than twist it. Twisting destroys the cells and makes the lettuce wilt. Lettuce smushers are tracked down relentlessly at Cabbagetown.

I must tell you about cabbage augury. If you cut a red cabbage in half through the stem end, you'll see a figure in the middle of the cabbage. That figure is either an angel or a devil. Just look carefully and you'll be able to tell. The cabbage angels, with halos and radiance, mean you'll have a good day. The devils, with horns and irregualr heads, mean watch out! This is serious. When we do salad gratings at the restaurant, we often keep cutting up cabbages until the angels outnumber the devils. That way everyone gets a good day.

If you add enough nuts, cheese, tofu, hard-boiled egg slices, croutons, etc., to a salad, the salad can be a main dish. Through the years we've served three main dish salads at Cabbagetown—the Wings of Life Salad, the Cascadilla Salad, and Darryl's Pasta Salad. Those recipes are at the beginning of the chapter. Other specialty salads follow.

Wings of Life Salad

2 cups Marinated Tofu (page 54)

6 cups steamed broccoli (page 55)

1 cup cashews

1/2 pound cheese (Cheddar, Swiss, feta, or cottage)

Salad greens and vegetables

Alfalfa sprouts, finely grated carrots, or finely grated beets

Your favorite Cabbagetown salad dressing (page 67–74)

One day after Steve and I had run Cabbagetown for about 2 years, Amy and I were discussing what we could do to expand the menu. "Why don't we serve the customers what the staff eats?" she suggested. Thus was born the Wings of Life Salad.

1. Prepare the tofu and the broccoli. Allow to cool.

2. Toast the cashews in a 350°F. oven or toaster oven for about 20 minutes, or until lightly browned. Be careful not to burn them.

3. Grate the Cheddar or Swiss cheese, or crumble the feta.

4. Prepare a base of salad greens, including any chopped or grated fresh vegetables you like.

5. Toss the tofu cubes, the steamed broccoli, the nuts, and the grated or crumbled cheeses into the salad greens. If you're using cottage cheese, put it on top of the salad greens around the edges. Top with alfalfa sprouts, grated carrots, or grated beets (or all 3).

6. At the last minute toss the salad with your choice of a Cabbagetown salad dressing and serve. Or serve the salad undressed and let each person put on his or her own dressing.

7. This salad is a whole meal. You might want to serve bread and butter or small cups of soup with it, but it can stand on its own.

Yield: Serves 4

Marinated Tofu

2 tablespoons light vegetable oil
1 pound tofu, cut in bite-size cubes (2 cups)
2 cloves of garlic, finely chopped
Freshly ground black pepper
1 teaspoon dried dill weed or 2 tablespoons
   finely chopped fresh dill
Pinch cayenne
1 teaspoon dark sesame oil
2 teaspoons tamari or soy sauce

This is the basic way we prepare tofu for use in salads and stir-fries. "Marinated" is a slight misnomer, but it conveys the idea. There's lots of flavor in the tofu cubes.

1. In a medium-size frying pan, heat the oil. Add the tofu cubes and fry for about 10 minutes, stirring frequently so nothing sticks.
2. Add the garlic, black pepper, dill, and cayenne. Continue frying and stirring until the cubes are lightly browned and crisp, about 5 minutes more.
3. Add the dark sesame oil and soy sauce, stir in, and turn off the heat.
4. Taste and adjust the seasonings.

Yield: 2 cups. Serves 4 in salads or stir-fries

Steamed Broccoli

Broccoli
Water

Here's how we steam broccoli for salads and stir-fries. The same technique works for cauliflower, green beans, asparagus, brussels sprouts, and any other dense vegetable you want to steam.

1. Cut the broccoli into bite-size pieces. Use the stem too. If you peel off the outside layer, the stem is edible except for a little woody portion right at the base.
2. Steam the broccoli pieces in a steaming basket over boiling water. (The pot should be covered.) Or blanch them by dropping them into a large frying pan filled with enough boiling water to cover them.
3. Steam or blanch the broccoli until it is *just tender*, about 5 minutes. The broccoli starts to smell sweeter when it's done. It will also feel tender when pierced with a knife. Catching the broccoli at just the right point is a real art.
4. As soon as the broccoli is cooked, pour it into a colander and run cold water over it to stop its cooking and keep it green.

Cascadilla Salad

1 pound tempeh
1 tablespoon tamari or soy sauce
3 tablespoons light vegetable oil
2 cups raw nuts and seeds
Salad greens
Several of your favorite fresh vegetables,
    lots of them, finely chopped
Alfalfa sprouts, finely grated carrots, or
    finely grated beets
Lemon Sesame Dressing (page 70)

1. Prepare the tempeh. Put it in boiling water to which you've added 1 tablespoon tamari or soy sauce. Return to a boil, then boil gently for 20 minutes. Pour through a colander to drain off the water. Cut the tempeh into bite-size cubes and fry in the oil until lightly browned and crisp on all sides. Or for the genuine Cabbagetown experience prepare the tempeh Alan's way (page 57).
2. Make the nuts and seeds into a meal by grinding them through a grain mill, or by blending them at low speed in a blender or food processor. Almonds are delicious. I also like pumpkin seeds and sunflower seeds.
3. Prepare a base of salad greens. Mix chopped fresh vegetables into it. We found that chopped daikon (Chinese radish) tastes good in this salad, as do regular radishes. We also like carrots, asparagus, zucchini, cauliflower, fresh green peas, everything! This salad must be filled with vegetables to earn its name.
4. Toss the tempeh cubes into the greens and vegetables. Cover with the nut and seed meal. Top with alfalfa sprouts, grated carrots, or grated beets (or all 3).
5. At the last minute toss with dressing and serve. Or let each person put on his or her own dressing.
6. This salad makes a whole meal. I can't think of anything you'd want with it except something to drink. Carrot juice, white wine, and beer all go nicely.

Yield: Serves 4

TEMPEH

1 pound tempeh
1 tablespoon tamari or soy sauce
3 tablespoons light vegetable oil

MOCK HOISIN SAUCE

1/2 cup tamari or soy sauce
1/4 cup honey
2 tablespoons red wine vinegar
1/2-inch piece fresh ginger, finely chopped
2 cloves of garlic, finely chopped
1 tablespoon arrowroot or cornstarch

When I put the Cascadilla Salad on the menu, I just wrote "with tempeh," and trusted that the staff would figure out a good way to prepare it. Sure enough, Alan came up with this delicious tempeh recipe.

1. Put the tempeh in boiling water to which you've added 1 tablespoon tamari or soy sauce. Return to a boil, then boil gently for 20 minutes. Pour through a colander to drain off the water.
2. Cut the tempeh into bite-size cubes. Fry in the oil until lightly browned and crisp on all sides.
3. Mix all the sauce ingredients in a small pot, and cook over low heat until thick, stirring frequently so the sauce will be smooth.
4. Toss the tempeh while still warm with the sauce.
5. Allow to cool.

Yield: Serves 4 in salad

Darryl's Pasta Salad

1 pound pasta
1 cup Tarragon Vinaigrette Dressing
(page 71)
1/2 teaspoon dried or finely chopped fresh
tarragon
1/4 teaspoon salt
1 1/2 cups Tamari-Roasted Almonds
(page 59)
1–2 cups freshly grated Parmesan cheese
Salad greens and vegetables
Alfalfa sprouts, finely grated carrots, or
finely grated beets
Black olives
Your favorite Cabbagetown salad dressing
(page 67–74)

Darryl is the name of our salad refrigerator at Cabbagetown. A friend named Darryl had been to a conference and pasted his name tag to the refrigerator. The tag stuck. When I noticed that every restaurant I visited in New York was serving a pasta salad, I invented this one for Cabbagetown. We use pasta shells because they form little pockets to catch the dressing.

1. Cook the pasta according to the instructions on page 109. After you've returned the pasta to the cooking pot, toss in the 1 cup of dressing, the tarragon, and the salt. Allow to cool, tossing occasionally to blend the flavors.
2. Prepare the almonds and grate the cheese.
3. Make a nest of your favorite salad greens and vegetables in a big salad bowl. If you want to go all out, sliced raw mushrooms, sliced red onions, and sliced avocados are good in this salad.
4. Put the pasta in the center of the greens. Cover with a thick layer of Parmesan cheese, then sprinkle with the almonds, the sprouts, grated carrots, or grated beets (or all 3), and the black olives.
5. Leave the salad this way for maximum scenic effect until you're ready to eat it. Then toss with your choice of a Cabbagetown salad dressing and serve. Or serve the salad undressed and let each person put on his or her own dressing.
6. This salad is good with crusty sourdough bread and a dry white wine or Zinfandel. Be sure to have the pepper grinder on the table.

Yield: Serves 4

Tamari-Roasted Almonds

1 1/2 cups almonds
2 tablespoons tamari or soy sauce

We use these flavorful almonds in salads and in stir-fried vegetable dishes. They're also good for nibbling.

1. Toast the almonds in a 350°F. oven or toaster oven for about 25 minutes, or until lightly browned.
2. Mix in the tamari or soy sauce.
3. Return to the oven for 5 minutes so the tamari can bake into the almonds. Do not bake any longer or the tamari will burn.
4. Use the roasted almonds whole or chop them in half.
5. These are best if served immediately, but they will stay crisp stored in a covered jar at room temperature for about a week.

Yield: 1 1/2 cups

Eve's Tabouli

2 cups bulgur
2 teaspoons salt
1 1/2 cups boiling water
1/2 cup olive oil
Juice of 2 lemons
2 cloves of garlic, finely chopped
1 onion, diced
1 green pepper, diced
1 cucumber, diced
1 tomato, diced
1 tablespoon finely chopped fresh
    peppermint or spearmint
1/2 cup finely chopped fresh parsley
1/2 teaspoon black pepper

The secret to this salad is the small amount of liquid, which leaves the bulgur flaky, not mushy.

1. In a large bowl, mix the bulgur with the salt, then add the boiling water. Cover for 20 minutes, stirring occasionally.
2. Add the oil and lemon juice and let sit another 10 minutes.
3. Toss in the chopped vegetables, mint, parsley, and pepper. Marinate the salad in the refrigerator for several hours before serving, tossing it occasionally so the whole salad is covered with dressing.
4. If you want the salad to be a whole meal, serve it with pita bread, black olives, and feta cheese.

Yield: Serves 4

Craig's Mexican Potato Salad

3 potatoes
4 tablespoons butter
2 cups fresh or frozen corn
1/2 cup cashews
1/2 cup sunflower seeds
1 tablespoon ground cumin
2 teaspoons ground coriander
1/4 cup sherry
1 onion, chopped
1 cup chopped black olives
1/4 cup finely chopped fresh chives or
  scallions
1 cup sour cream
1 teaspoon salt

This is another of Craig's marvelous inventions. It's very good plain, as a dip for tortilla chips, or with cheese melted over it on tostadas.

1. Scrub the potatoes well, but do not peel. Cook in water to cover until just tender, about 30 minutes after the water boils. Do not overcook. The easiest way to tell if a potato is done is to spear it with a knife. Dice into bite-size cubes.
2. Cook the vegetables in 2 steps to avoid overcooking anything, and to ensure the separate, crisp texture of each salad ingredient. Melt half the butter in a medium-size frying pan. Add the corn, cashews, sunflower seeds, and half the spices. Sauté for 4–5 minutes, until the corn is lightly cooked. Mix in half the sherry. Remove to a large bowl.
3. Melt the remaining butter in the frying pan. Add the onion, the cooked potato cubes, and the remaining spices. Sauté until the onions are tender. Mix in the rest of the sherry. Add to the other vegetables in the bowl.
4. While the vegetables are still hot, mix in the olives, chives or scallions, sour cream, and salt. Taste and reseason if necessary.
5. Serve immediately or store in the refrigerator until serving.

Yield: Serves 4

Din's New England Potato Salad

6 potatoes
1/2 cup Tarragon Vinaigrette Dressing
  (page 71)
4 hard-boiled eggs, diced
3 celery stalks, diced
1 red or white onion, diced
1/2 cup chopped green olives or 2
  tablespoons capers
About 1 cup mayonnaise or Rugged Garlic
  Dressing (page 68)
Salt and pepper to taste
Paprika

Din and David, two major figures in the history of Cabbagetown, maintained that all our food was too elaborate. They leaned toward the simple, straightforward foods of their New England heritage. Here is Din's New England Potato Salad recipe. She'll think it's too bad and typical that I've jazzed it up a little with onions and green olives.

1. Scrub the potatoes well, but do not peel. Cook in water to cover until just tender, about 30 minutes after the water boils. Dice into bite-size cubes. Toss with the 1/2 cup of dressing and allow to cool thoroughly.
2. In a large bowl, mix together the potatoes, eggs, celery, onion, and olives or capers. Add enough mayonnaise or garlic dressing to make the salad moist but not mushy.
3. Add salt and pepper to taste. Chill thoroughly.
4. Sprinkle with paprika before serving.

Yield: Serves 4

Robin's French Lentil Salad

1 cup uncooked lentils
3 cups water
1 bay leaf
1 tablespoon olive oil
1/3 cup Tarragon Vinaigrette Dressing
(page 71)
1/2 teaspoon dried or finely chopped fresh
thyme
1 firm ripe tomato, diced
Salt and pepper to taste
Salad greens

There is always one Cabbagetown employee who has lived in France and loves everything French. Robin lived with a French family in Grenoble. This simple salad was one of their favorites.

1. Measure the lentils, water, bay leaf, and olive oil into a medium-size pot. Bring to a boil, then turn down the heat and simmer, uncovered, for about 30 minutes, or until the water is totally absorbed. Turn off the heat, and leave for 30 minutes to allow the lentils to settle. It's important that the lentils be as firm and whole as possible for this salad.
2. Toss with the dressing, thyme, and tomato, being careful not to mush the lentils.
3. Add salt and pepper to taste. Chill thoroughly.
4. Serve on a bed of greens as a side salad. This is especially good with some crusty bread and butter and an omelette.

Yield: Serves 4

Cabbagetown Cole Slaw

1 large wedge red cabbage (4 cups chopped)
2 carrots or 1/4 butternut squash
1 onion, slivered in thin crescents (optional)
3/4 cup almonds or hazelnuts, coarsely chopped
Rugged Garlic Dressing (page 68)
2 tablespoons prepared horseradish
Freshly ground black pepper

This is a basic cabbage salad with a few Cabbagetown twists.

1. Chop the cabbage into medium-size shreds. (We like the texture of chopped cabbage better than grated.)
2. Peel and grate the carrots. If you'd like to try raw butternut squash, it's a little richer and sweeter that carrots, and delicious. Peel the squash, take out the seeds, and grate.
3. In a large bowl, mix together the cabbage, carrots or squash, and the onion if you're using it. Mix in the nuts.
4. Toss with enough garlic dressing to coat the salad thoroughly. Mix in the horseradish and black pepper.
5. Taste. If the salad is slightly lacking in flavor, try adding more dressing or a little salt.
6. Serve as a side salad or as the basis for the C-Town Special Sandwich (page 146).

Yield: Serves 4

Salad Dressings

Customers often ask which of our salad dressings is our house dressing. They all are. However, I've found that most Cabbagetown customers and employees are addicted to one dressing. The adventurous start out eating Rugged Garlic, the timid Yoghurt-Tahini, the health-oriented Lemon Sesame Dressing. You can serve raw vegetables with our dressings as dips; you can make beautifully arranged salads on plates or platters or boards, and douse them with our dressings; or you can make magnificent tossed salads and at the last minute pour on your favorite dressing.

Yoghurt-Tahini Dressing

1 cup plain yoghurt
1/2 cup tahini
Juice of 1/2 lemon
1 clove of garlic, finely chopped
1/4 teaspoon salt
2 tablespoons finely chopped fresh parsley
1 tablespoon finely chopped fresh chives or
scallions (optional)

Yoghurt-Tahini has been the faithful salad dressing at Cabbagetown from the first day my partner and I bought the restaurant. We also use it as a dip for raw and steamed vegetables when we cater parties, and as a dressing for sandwiches in pita bread.

1. With a whisk, mix together all the ingredients until smooth.
2. Taste on a vegetable stick. You might want to add more lemon juice.
3. Try crumbled feta cheese in any tossed salad with this dressing.

Yield: 1 1/2 cups

Rugged Garlic Dressing

1 egg
1/2 teaspoon salt
1 tablespoon red wine vinegar
4–6 cloves of garlic
1 cup light vegetable oil
1/4 cup red wine vinegar
1/2 cup lightly packed fresh green herbs
  (chives, scallions, parsley, basil, dill)
1/2 teaspoon black pepper

This is the dressing customers make jokes about. "Oh dear," a young Cornell student will say glancing at her boyfriend. "I'll have the garlic dressing if you do."

1. If you're using a whisk, finely chop the garlic and the fresh green herbs. If you're using a blender, you can add them whole and the blender will chop them.
2. Whisk or blend the egg with the salt, 1 tablespoon vinegar, and the garlic until creamy.
3. Whisking or blending constantly, add about 1/2–2/3 cup of the oil in a slow trickle. At some point the dressing will take and become much thicker.
4. After it thickens, continue beating in the remaining oil alternately with the 1/4 cup vinegar.
5. Whisk or blend in the herbs and pepper.
6. Taste on a vegetable stick and adjust the seasonings if needed.
7. This dressing tastes especially good on salads with croutons and big leaves of fresh spinach.
8. If the dressing doesn't take—that is, if it breaks into separate oil and vinegar layers—whisk or blend another egg and add the dressing to the egg, whisking or blending constantly as you did with the oil. If this still doesn't work, just use the dressing as it is. It will have the consistency of a vinaigrette.

Yield: 1 1/2 cups

Steve's Tofu Dressing

1/2 cup crumbled tofu
1/4 cup water
2 tablespoons tahini
2 tablespoons light vegetable oil
2 tablespoons red wine vinegar
1 tablespoon tamari or soy sauce
1 teaspoon dried dill weed or 1 tablespoon
   finely chopped fresh dill
1 teaspoon dark sesame oil
1 clove of garlic, finely chopped

This creamy dressing is subtly flavored with dark sesame oil, tahini, and dill. It's a good way to introduce people to tofu.

1. Measure all the ingredients into the blender and blend until smooth.
2. Taste on a vegetable stick and adjust the seasonings if needed.

Yield: 1 cup

Lemon Sesame Dressing

1/4 cup sesame seeds
1 cup light vegetable oil
Juice of 2 lemons
2 tablespoons red wine vinegar
1 tablespoon tamari or soy sauce
1 cup lightly packed fresh green herbs
   (chives, scallions, parsley, basil, dill)
1/2 teaspoon salt
1/2 teaspoon mustard powder
1 teaspoon dried thyme or finely chopped
   fresh thyme
1/4 teaspoon dried or fresh whole
   rosemary

Do you remember that I said everyone is addicted to one Cabbagetown dressing? Lemon Sesame Dressing is light and fresh, and I can't resist the sesame flavor. Our abbreviation for this dressing when taking orders is "LSD." Customers love it when they get their checks.

1. Toast the sesame seeds over low heat in a frying pan until they're lightly browned. Be careful not to burn them.
2. Measure all the ingredients including the toasted sesame seeds into the blender and blend until smooth.
3. Taste on a vegetable stick and adjust the seasonings if needed.

Yield: 2 cups

Tarragon Vinaigrette Dressing

3/4 cup olive oil
Juice of 1 lemon
1 tablespoon red wine vinegar
1 tablespoon prepared French mustard
2 cloves of garlic, finely chopped
1 teaspoon dried tarragon or 1/2 teaspoon
   finely chopped fresh tarragon
1/2 teaspoon salt
1/2 teaspoon freshly ground black pepper

This is a very simple dressing. Because it is so simple, the quality of the ingredients you use makes a big difference. Get the best olive oil and the best French mustard you can. If you can find it, fresh tarragon is better than dried.

1. Mix together all the ingredients.
2. Taste on a vegetable stick and adjust the seasonings if needed.
3. This dressing tastes especially good on salads with one or more of the following ingredients: avocados, cooked lentils, tender lettuces, crumbled bleu cheese, croutons, or cooked pasta.

Yield: 1 cup

Bleu Cheese Dressing

2 cups sour cream
1/4 pound bleu cheese, crumbled (1 cup)
1/4 teaspoon salt
1/2 teaspoon freshly ground black pepper
Juice of 1/2 lemon
1/4 cup finely chopped fresh chives or
   scallions

This dressing has lemon juice and chives or scallions for extra flavor. We also use it as a dip for carrot sticks, raw mushrooms, whole scallions, and steamed broccoli.

1. Mix together all the ingredients.
2. Allow it to sit in the refrigerator for an hour or more before serving so the flavors can blend. Taste on a vegetable stick and adjust the seasonings if needed.

Yield: 3 cups

Robin and Din washing lettuce

Jane's Buttermilk Dressing

1/2 cup mayonnaise or Rugged Garlic
  Dressing (page 68)
1/2 cup buttermilk
2 cloves of garlic, finely chopped
1 tablespoon finely chopped fresh chives or
  scallions
1/4 cup finely chopped fresh parsley
2 tablespoons finely chopped fresh dill
  (optional)
Salt and pepper to taste

This is rather like a ranch dressing with lots of fresh parsley. It's light—excellent for all tossed salads.

1. Mix together all the ingredients except the salt and pepper.
2. Add salt and pepper, tasting the dressing on a vegetable stick.
3. Jane's dressing tastes especially good on salads with sliced hard-boiled eggs and sliced raw mushrooms.

Yield: 1 1/2 cups

Soups

When I wrote Wings of Life *I said, "There is one soup," and I meant it. The one and only soup to me was a thick tomato and vegetable stew, very like the Minestrone I cooked on my first day at Cabbagetown. After we owned the restaurant, I suddenly realized that Split Pea Soup had a unique and worthwhile identity. Black Bean Soup came next. Soon after that I was in there inventing new soups with the best of my cooks—Norwegian Cream of Cabbage Soup, Eddy Street Onion Soup...*

We spend as many hours discussing what to name our soups as we spend creating them. My all-time favorite name is "Amy's Transatlantic Cream of Lima Bean Soup," which was invented on Columbus Day. Unfortunately the recipe for that one is lost in history. But many of our other soup recipes have survived and have been made over and over. I've cut the best of them down from huge five gallon pots to home-size quantities.

The soup recipes are in four categories: bean soups (which I think are our best), cream soups, miscellaneous hot soups, and cold soups.

Split Pea Soup

2 cups uncooked green split peas
1/3 cup uncooked barley
10 cups water
2 bay leaves
2 tablespoons light vegetable oil
1 onion, finely chopped
1 carrot, finely chopped
2 cloves of garlic, finely chopped
1 teaspoon dried or finely chopped fresh
   thyme
1 teaspoon salt

This savory soup is very simple to make. It's wonderful to make and eat on a cold and rainy day.

1. Measure the split peas, barley, water, and bay leaves into a soup pot. Bring to a boil, then reduce the heat and simmer, partially covered, stirring occasionally to keep the peas from sticking. Cook for about 45 minutes, or until the peas and barley are tender.
2. Heat the oil in a separate frying pan. Add the onion, carrot, garlic, and thyme, and sauté until the carrot pieces are tender.
3. Add the cooked vegetables to the split peas, along with the salt. Continue simmering for at least 30 minutes to blend the flavors, stirring frequently.
4. Taste and adjust the seasonings. Some people like to add black pepper to this soup.

Yield: Serves 6

Black Bean Soup

2 cups uncooked black beans, sorted for stones and rinsed

8 cups water (or combination water and olive juice)

2 bay leaves

1/4 cup olive oil

2 onions, finely chopped

2 green peppers, finely chopped

4 cloves of garlic, finely chopped

1 tablespoon ground cumin

1 teaspoon dried or finely chopped fresh oregano

1 teaspoon mustard powder

1 teaspoon dried dill weed or 1 tablespoon finely chopped fresh dill

1/2 cup chopped green olives

1 teaspon salt

Juice of 1 lemon

Sour cream (optional)

One day at lunch a customer came back to our kitchen and said, "Your soup is okay, but black bean soup is the staple in the country I come from. Let me show you how to make it great." This is her recipe. Part of the secret is the green olives.

1. Measure the black beans, water (or water and olive juice), and bay leaves into a soup pot. Bring to a boil, then reduce the heat and simmer, partially covered, stirring occasionally to keep the beans from sticking. Cook for about 2 hours, or until the beans are soft.

2. In a separate frying pan, heat the olive oil. Add the onions, green peppers, and garlic and sauté until limp and lightly browned. Add the spices and herbs. Sauté for a few minutes, adding more oil if necessary to keep from sticking. Add the olives and cook 5 minutes.

3. Using a potato masher or a bean masher or a fork, mash about 1/4 of the beans into a paste to give the soup a good thick texture. You can do this in the soup pot or remove the beans, mash them, and return.

4. Add the cooked vegetables to the beans, along with the salt and the lemon juice. Continue simmering for as long as possible.

5. Taste and adjust the seasonings. You might want to add more salt.

6. Serve plain or top each bowl with a dollop of sour cream.

Yield: Serves 6

Spinach Lentil Soup

1 cup uncooked lentils
1/3 cup uncooked green split peas
7 cups water
2 bay leaves
2 potatoes
2 tablespoons olive oil
2 onions, finely chopped
2 cloves of garlic, finely chopped
1 tablespoon dried dill weed or 2
    tablespoons finely chopped fresh dill
1/2 teaspoon black pepper
8–10 ounces fresh spinach or Swiss chard,
    finely chopped (6 cups)
1 teaspoon salt
2 tablespoons red wine vinegar

As a restaurant cook, you go through periods of using one ingredient in everything you make. I invented this soup during my lentil phase. It has become one of our staple soups.

1. Measure the lentils, split peas, water, and bay leaves into a soup pot. Bring to a boil, then reduce the heat and simmer, partially covered, stirring occasionally to keep the lentils and peas from sticking. Cook for about 30 minutes, or until the lentils are tender.
2. Scrub the potatoes well but do not peel. Dice in small cubes and cook in water to cover until the cubes are cooked but still firm, about 5 minutes after the water boils.
3. In a separate frying pan, heat the olive oil. Add the onions and sauté for a minute or two; then add the garlic, dill, and pepper. Sauté a few minutes more. Add part of the spinach. Wait for it to wilt, then add more. Continue in this fashion until all the spinach is in the pan and lightly cooked.
4. Add the potatoes, potato water, and the spinach mixture to the lentils, along with the salt. Continue to simmer for at least 30 minutes to blend the flavors, stirring frequently.
5. About 10 minutes before serving, mix in the vinegar. (Vinegar enhances the flavor of many bean soups. It's better than lemon juice because vinegar adds a deep, sweet flavor as well as tartness, whereas lemon juice makes the beans bitter.)Cook 10 minutes more, then taste and adjust the seasonings.

Yield: Serves 6

Roger's Minestrone for Complete Idiots

1/2 cup uncooked chick-peas or kidney
   beans (2 cups cooked)
6 cups water
2 bay leaves
1/4 cup olive oil
2 onions, diced
4 cloves of garlic, finely chopped
2 green peppers, diced
1/2 teaspoon dried or finely chopped fresh
   oregano
2 teaspoons dried basil or 2 tablespoons
   finely chopped fresh basil
1 teaspoon dried marjoram or 1 tablespoon
   finely chopped fresh marjoram
1 teaspoon dried or finely chopped fresh
   thyme
1 teaspoon salt
Freshly ground pepper, as much as you like
1 potato, diced
2 carrots, diced
2 stalks broccoli, diced
1 wedge green cabbage, cut in bite-size
   chunks (4 cups)
2 quarts canned tomatoes
1/2 cup red wine
1/4 cup finely chopped parsley

Roger came from California and helped us get the restaurant moving shortly after Steve and I bought it. The recipe is named after *The Volkswagen Book for Complete Idiots*, one of the bibles at Cabbagetown since we all had Volkswagens. The idea of the Volkswagen book was that with good instructions and a good attitude everyone can fix cars. Roger's idea was that everyone can cook.
THIS MAKES A BIG POT OF SOUP.

1. Measure the chick-peas or kidney beans, water, and bay leaves into a medium-size pot. Bring to a boil, then reduce the heat and simmer, partially covered, for about 2–3 hours, or until the beans are tender.
2. In a soup pot, heat the olive oil. Toss in the onions and garlic, and sauté for about 5 minutes. Add the peppers and sauté for 5 minutes more. Reduce the heat and add the herbs, salt, and pepper. Sauté for 5 minutes more, stirring frequently to keep it from sticking.
3. Add the other vegetables one at a time, letting each vegetable cook down as you chop the next one. If the vegetables start to stick, add a bit of juice from the tomatoes. You can add any other vegetables you like. Zucchini, green peas, corn, and chopped fresh spinach are especially good.
4. Crush the canned tomatoes with your hand or the back of a spoon to get small pieces. Add the tomatoes to the soup and simmer for 15 minutes. Add the wine and continue to simmer.
5. When the beans are tender, add them to

the soup pot, along with the bean cooking water. Add the parsley. Dilute to good serving consistency with water, stock, or tomato juice. Continue to simmer for 30–60 minutes to blend the flavors.

6. Taste and reseason. Serve as is or sprinkle each bowl with grated Parmesan, Swiss, or Cheddar cheese.

Yield: Serves 12

Swedish Split Pea Soup

2 cups uncooked yellow split peas
8 cups water
2 bay leaves
2 potatoes
2 tablespoons butter
2 onions, finely chopped
2 cloves of garlic, finely chopped
2 teaspoons dried marjoram or 1
   tablespoon finely chopped fresh
   marjoram
1 teaspoon dried or fresh whole rosemary,
   slightly crushed in your hands
1 teaspoon salt

This soup is made from yellow split peas and potatoes. The addition of marjoram gives it a special taste.

1. Measure the split peas, water, and bay leaves into a soup pot. Bring to a boil, then reduce the heat and simmer, partially covered, stirring occasionally to keep the peas from sticking. Cook for about 45 minutes, or until the peas are tender.

2. Meanwhile scrub the potatoes well but do not peel. Dice in small cubes and cook in water to cover until the cubes are cooked but still firm, about 5 minutes after the water boils.

3. In a separate frying pan, heat the butter. Add the onions and sauté for 4–5 minutes, until the onions are translucent. Don't overcook the onions; a light and fresh onion flavor is best in this soup. Add the garlic, marjoram, and rosemary, and sauté a few minutes more.

4. Add the potatoes, the potato water, and the cooked vegetables to the split peas, along with the salt. Continue simmering for at least 30 minutes to blend the flavors, stirring frequently.

5. Taste and adjust the seasonings.

6. To follow the Scandinavian tradition serve this soup on Thursdays, with homemade bread or rye crackers, unsalted butter, mustard, and Jarlsberg cheese.

Yield: Serves 6

Cabbage Dal

1 cup uncooked red lentils
3 cups water
2 bay leaves
1/4 cup light vegetable oil
2 teaspoons black mustard seeds
1/4 teaspoon asafetida
1 fresh hot pepper, finely chopped
4 cloves of garlic, finely chopped
1/2-inch piece fresh ginger, finely chopped
1 teaspoon turmeric
2 onions, chopped
1 wedge green cabbage, finely chopped
  (4 cups)
1 quart canned tomatoes
2 teaspoons salt
1 teaspoon molasses
5 teaspoons ground cumin
4 teaspoons ground coriander
1/4 teaspoon cayenne
Juice of 1 lemon

Varsha, our Indian cooking guru, suggested this as the perfect Indian soup for the restaurant. It's thick with cabbage and red lentils and very flavorful.

1. Measure the lentils, water, and bay leaves into a medium-size pot. Bring to a boil, then reduce the heat and simmer, partially covered, stirring occasionally to keep the lentils from sticking. Cook for about 20 minutes, or until the lentils are soft.
2. In a soup pot, heat the oil. When you drop a mustard seed in the hot oil and it sizzles, the temperature is right. Pour in the mustard seeds and cook until they pop. Lower the heat and stir frequently so you don't burn any of the seeds. Stir in the asafetida, then the chopped hot pepper, then the garlic and ginger, then the turmeric. Cook for 3–4 minutes, stirring frequently.
3. Add the onions. Stir and cook for 10 minutes. Add the cabbage. Cook for 15 minutes.
4. Crush the canned tomatoes with your hand or the back of a spoon to get small pieces. Add to the soup, along with the accompanying tomato juice, the salt, and the molasses. Cook for 20 minutes, or until hot. Stir frequently so nothing sticks.
5. Stir in the ground cumin, coriander, and cayenne. Add the cooked lentils and water. Continue simmering for at least 30 minutes to blend the flavors. Add the lemon juice.
6. Taste and adjust the seasonings.

Yield: Serves 6

Indian Lentil Soup

1 1/2 cups uncooked lentils
4 cups water
2 bay leaves
1/4 cup light vegetable oil
2 tablespoons black mustard seeds
2 tablespoons cumin seeds
1/4 teaspoon asafetida
1 fresh hot pepper, finely chopped
4 cloves of garlic, finely chopped
1/2 inch piece fresh ginger, finely chopped
1 teaspoon turmeric
2 onions, chopped
1/2 cup dried unsweetened or grated fresh
  coconut
1 tablespoon light vegetable oil
1 quart canned tomatoes
2 teaspoons salt
2 tablespoons ground cumin
2 tablespoons ground coriander
1/4 teaspoon cayenne

This soup has that genuine Indian taste you don't often find in American versions of Indian food.

1. Measure the lentils, water, and bay leaves into a medium-size pot. Bring to a boil, then reduce the heat and simmer, partially covered, stirring occasionally to keep the lentils from sticking. Cook for about 30 minutes, or until the lentils are tender.

2. In a soup pot, heat the oil. When you drop a mustard seed in the hot oil and it sizzles, the temperature is right. Pour in the mustard seeds and cumin seeds, and cook until most of them pop. Lower the heat and stir frequently so you don't burn any of the seeds. Stir in the asafetida, then the chopped hot pepper, then the garlic and ginger, then the turmeric. Cook for 3–4 minutes, stirring frequently.

3. Add the onions. Stir and cook for 10 minutes. Add the coconut along with 1 tablespoon oil, then cook for 10 minutes more.

4. Crush the canned tomatoes with your hand or the back of a spoon to get small pieces. Add to the soup, along with the accompanying tomato juice and the salt. Cook for 20 minutes, or until hot. Stir frequently so nothing sticks.

5. Stir in the ground cumin, coriander, and cayenne. Add the cooked lentils and water. Continue to simmer for at least 30 minutes.

SPROUTED INDIAN LENTIL SOUP

Use sprouted lentils for an extraordinarily flavorful, light, and nutritious soup. Start with 1 cup of uncooked lentils. Sprout them for 3 days. Don't cook them—just add them to the soup at step 5 along with 1 cup water. Continue simmering as usual.

INDIAN BEAN SOUPS

Try this recipe with other types of beans. We especially like aduki beans.

Yield: Serves 6

Indian Spinach and Peanut Soup

2 potatoes
8–10 ounces fresh spinach or Swiss chard,
   chopped (6 cups)
4 cups water
2 cups peanuts, raw or roasted
1/4 cup light vegetable oil
4 teaspoons cumin seeds
4 cloves of garlic, finely chopped
1 fresh hot pepper, finely chopped
1/4 teaspoon asafetida
1 teaspoon turmeric
2 teaspoons salt
1 teaspoon ground cumin
1 teaspoon ground coriander
1/4 teaspoon cayenne
1/2 cup sour cream
1/2 cup yoghurt

This is another unique soup. Varsha said when her sister was pregnant this was all she wanted to eat.

1. Scrub the potatoes well but do not peel. Dice in small cubes. Put in a large pot. Put the chopped spinach on top and pour in the water. Bring the water to a boil, then reduce the heat and simmer, covered, for about 15 minutes, or until the potatoes are cooked.
2. Meanwhile, make the peanuts into roasted peanut meal. If you are starting with raw peanuts, roast them in a dry skillet for about 10 minutes, or until dark spots appear. Stir frequently so the peanuts don't burn. Allow to cool. Grind them in a grain mill, or at low speed in a blender or food processor. Don't grind too fast or you will make peanut butter. If you are starting with roasted peanuts, grind them as above.
3. In a soup pot, heat the oil. Add the cumin seeds and garlic. When the garlic is cooked to a light brown color, add the hot pepper, then the asafetida, then the turmeric. Cook for 3–4 minutes.
4. Add the cooked potatoes, spinach, and water. Stir well. Then add the salt, ground cumin, coriander, and cayenne.
5. Add the peanut meal. Cook for 15 minutes to blend the flavors.
6. Remove a little hot soup from the pot and stir the yoghurt and sour cream into it. Return it to the rest of the soup. Simmer for 15 minutes, stirring frequently.

Yield: Serves 6

Cream of Zucchini Soup

3 tablespoons butter
1 onion, finely chopped
2 cloves of garlic, finely chopped
2 teaspoons dried basil or 1 tablespoon
   finely chopped fresh basil
1/2 teaspoon dried or finely chopped fresh
   tarragon
1/2 teaspoon dried or finely chopped fresh
   thyme
1/4–1/2 teaspoon black pepper
1 teaspoon salt
2 medium-size zucchini, cut in bite-size
   pieces (6 cups)
4 tablespoons butter
4 tablespoons whole wheat pastry flour
4–6 cups milk

This is a recipe for a cream soup thickened with a flour roux. It is elegant, rich, and buttery.

1. In a soup pot, melt 3 tablespoons butter. Add the onion and garlic and sauté until lightly browned. Add the herbs, pepper, and salt and cook for 2–3 minutes, stirring frequently. Add the zucchini and sauté until tender. Add a little water if necessary to keep the zucchini from sticking.

2. Make the roux in a separate pot. Melt 4 tablespoons butter. Mix in the flour with a whisk, 1 tablespoon at a time. Cook for about 1 minute, whisking constantly, to cook out the raw taste of the flour. Slowly add 2 cups of the milk, whisking constantly. Bring the mixture to a gentle boil, then reduce the heat, and simmer for about 5 minutes to thicken. Whisk frequently.

3. Pour the thickened milk over the vegetables in the soup pot. Slowly add more milk until a good serving consistency is reached. Heat gently until it simmers, then simmer for 5 minutes to thicken the soup and blend the flavors. Stir frequently.

4. Taste and adjust the seasonings.

CREAM OF VEGETABLE SOUP I
Substitute 6 cups of any chopped vegetable you like for the zucchini. I especially recommend asparagus, fiddlehead ferns, leeks, mushrooms, and onions.

Yield: Serves 6

Cream of Broccoli Soup

2 potatoes
2 bay leaves
3 tablespoons butter
1 onion, coarsely chopped
2 cloves of garlic, finely chopped
2 teaspoons dried marjoram or 1
   tablespoon finely chopped fresh
   marjoram
2 teaspoons dried basil or 1 tablespoon
   finely chopped fresh basil
1/2 teaspoon dried or finely chopped fresh
   thyme
1/4–1/2 teaspoon black pepper
1 teaspoon salt
1 medium-size head of broccoli
2–4 cups milk
2 tablespoons butter

We experimented and came up with this light cream soup thickened with blended potatoes. It doesn't curdle. This is a core recipe, with variations following.

1. Scrub the potatoes well but do not peel. Cook in water to cover with bay leaves until well done, about 30 minutes after the water boils. Remove the bay leaves.
2. In a soup pot, melt 3 tablespoons butter. Add the onion and garlic and sauté until golden brown. Add the herbs, pepper, and salt and cook for 2–3 minutes, stirring frequently.
3. Reserve about 2 cups of nice-looking broccoli florets. Coarsely chop the remaining broccoli, including the non-woody portions of the stem. Add to the onions and continue to sauté until the broccoli is limp and luscious. You want to cook the vegetables very thoroughly for blended cream soups because thorough cooking enhances the deeper and sweeter aspects of their flavor. Whenever the broccoli starts to stick, add potato water.
4. In 2 batches, blend the broccoli mixture, the potatoes, and the potato water with enough milk to reach a good serving consistency. Set aside in a bowl.
5. Chop the nice-looking broccoli you saved from step 3 into small bite-size pieces. In the soup pot, melt the remaining 2 tablespoons butter. Add the broccoli and sauté until the broccoli is soft but not overcooked. This broccoli will add texture to the soup.
6. Return the blended mixture to the soup pot. Heat gently to a serving temperature.

CREAM OF VEGETABLE SOUP II

Substitute 6–8 cups of your favorite vegetable for the broccoli and use your favorite herbs. Be sure to reserve 2 cups of chopped vegetables to add in step 5. Cauliflower, spinach, fresh green peas, and celery make tasty cream soups.

CREAM OF CAULIFLOWER SOUP WITH GREEN PEAS

Make Cream of Cauliflower Soup by substituting cauliflower for the broccoli. Add 2 cups of fresh or frozen green peas at step 5, after you have sautéed the small pieces of cauliflower for about 5 minutes. Sauté 2–3 minutes more, or until the cauliflower is tender and the peas are lightly cooked. Then proceed with the soup. This recipe is requested frequently at the restaurant.

Yield: Serves 6

Mushroom Chowder

2 potatoes
3 tablespoons butter
8–12 ounces mushrooms, thinly sliced
1 onion, finely chopped
2 cloves of garlic, finely chopped
1 carrot, finely diced
3 celery stalks, finely diced
1/2 teaspoon dried marjoram or 2
   teaspoons finely chopped fresh marjoram
1/2 teaspoon dried or finely chopped fresh
   thyme
1/2 teaspoon dried basil or 2 teaspoons
   finely chopped fresh basil
1/4 teaspoon paprika
1 teaspoon salt
1/4 teaspoon black pepper
2 bay leaves
3 tablespoons butter
3 tablespoons whole wheat pastry flour
2–3 cups milk

This rich vegetable chowder is thickened with a flour roux. It's just delicious.

1. Scrub the potatoes well but do not peel. Dice in small cubes and cook in water to cover until the cubes are cooked but still firm, about 5 minutes after the water boils.
2. In a soup pot, melt 3 tablespoons butter. Add the mushrooms and sauté over high heat until the mushrooms are lightly browned and flavorful. Reduce the heat, and add the onion, garlic, carrot, and celery. Cook until the vegetables are tender but not too soft. Add the herbs, paprika, salt, pepper, and bay leaves and cook for 2–3 minutes. Add a little potato water if the mixture starts to stick.
3. Add the cooked potatoes and water to the soup pot.
4. Make the roux in a separate pot. Melt 3 tablespoons butter. Mix in the flour with a whisk, 1 tablespoon at a time. Cook for about 1 minute, whisking constantly, to cook out the raw taste of the flour. Slowly add 2 cups of the milk, whisking constantly. Bring the mixture to a gentle boil, then reduce the heat, and simmer for about 5 minutes to thicken. Whisk frequently.
5. Pour the thickened milk over the vegetables in the soup pot. Slowly add more milk until a good serving consistency is reached. Heat gently until simmering, then simmer for 5 minutes to thicken the soup and blend the flavors.
6. Taste and adjust the seasonings.

Yield: Serves 6

Corn Chowder

3 potatoes
3 tablespoons butter
1 onion, finely diced
2 cloves of garlic, finely chopped
1 carrot, finely diced
3 celery stalks, finely diced
2 cups fresh or frozen corn
1/2 teaspoon dried marjoram or 2
   teaspoons finely chopped fresh marjoram
1/2 teaspoon dried or finely chopped fresh
   thyme
1/4 teaspoon paprika
1/4 teaspoon black pepper
1 teaspoon salt
2–3 cups milk
Chives or parsley for garnish (optional)

This is from Aunt June, Cabbagetown's best chowder cook.

1. Scrub the potatoes well but do not peel. Cook in water to cover until the potatoes are cooked but still firm, about 30 minutes after the water boils.
2. In a soup pot, melt the butter. Add the onion, garlic, carrot, and celery and sauté until the vegetables are cooked but not too soft. Add the corn and cook for 10 minutes more. Add the herbs, spices, and salt and cook for 3–4 minutes more.
3. Dice 1 1/2 potatoes into small cubes. Add to the soup pot.
4. Blend the remaining 1 1/2 potatoes with the potato water and 2–3 cups milk, enough to make a good serving consistency.
5. Add the blended mixture to the soup pot. Heat gently to a serving temperature.
6. Taste and adjust the seasonings. Garnish with finely chopped chives or parsley.

Yield: Serves 6

Norwegian Cream of Cabbage Soup

2 potatoes
2 tablespoons butter
1 onion, coarsely chopped
4 teaspoons caraway seeds
1/2 medium-size green cabbage (8 cups
    chopped)
2 cups milk
2 tablespoons butter
1 teaspoon salt
1/4 teaspoon black pepper
2 teaspoons cider vinegar

This is a thick potato and cabbage soup, with the slightly spicy flavor of caraway.

1. Scrub the potatoes well but do not peel. Cook in water to cover until well done, about 30 minutes after the water boils.
2. In a soup pot, melt 2 tablespoons butter. Add the onion and sauté until golden brown and sweet, about 10 minutes. Add the caraway seeds and sauté for 1 minute.
3. Coarsely chop two-thirds of the cabbage (including the cores). Add to the soup pot. To speed the cooking you might want to add the cabbage a little at a time and let it cook down, or add it all at once and cover the pot. Cook until the cabbage is sweet and limp.
4. Blend the onion-cabbage mixture with the potatoes, potato water, and milk. Set aside.
5. Finely chop the remaining cabbage. In the soup pot, melt 2 tablespoons butter. Add the remaining cabbage and sauté until the cabbage is limp.
6. Add the blended mixture to the soup pot, along with the salt, pepper, and vinegar. Heat gently until simmering, then simmer for 5–10 minutes to blend the flavors.
7. Taste and adjust the seasonings.

Yield: Serves 6

Cream of Butternut Squash Soup

2 potatoes
4 tablespoons butter
1 onion, chopped
1/4 teaspoon nutmeg
3/4 teaspoon cinnamon
3/4 teaspoon dried marjoram or 1 1/2
   teapoons finely chopped fresh marjoram
1/2 teaspoon salt
1 medium-size butternut squash (2 pounds)
2 tablespoons cream sherry
2 cups milk
1–2 teaspoons honey (optional)

1. Scrub the potatoes well but do not peel. Cook in water to cover until well done, about 30 minutes after the water boils.

2. In a soup pot, melt the butter. Add the onion and sauté until golden brown and sweet, about 10 minutes. Add the spices, marjoram, and salt and sauté for 2–3 minutes.

3. Peel the squash. A vegetable peeler works best. Remove the seeds and chop the squash into cubes. Add it to the onion and butter, along with a little potato water, and let it cook until *well done*, about 30–40 minutes. Cover the pot to speed the cooking, and stir occasionally. If it starts to stick, add more potato water.

4. Add the potatoes and potato water to the soup pot and cook together for about 10 minutes to blend the flavors.

5. Blend the squash mixture with the sherry and milk until smooth. If you don't have a blender, mash the squash mixture with a potato masher, then slowly mix in the sherry and milk.

6. Heat the soup gently until you're ready to serve it.

7. Taste and adjust the seasonings. The quality of the squash you started with will make a big difference in the final taste of the soup. Homegrown well-ripened squash is the sweetest. If your squash is not too sweet, you might want to add 1–2 teaspoons of honey to your soup to highlight the squash taste.

Yield: Serves 6

Potato Leek Soup

3 tablespoons butter
2 onions, chopped
1 teaspoon salt
1/2 teaspoon black pepper
Pinch nutmeg
2 big leeks, chopped, greens and all, or 2
   cups chopped wild leeks or scallions
2 celery stalks, chopped
2 cups water
4 potatoes, scrubbed and thinly sliced
4 cups milk
Finely chopped chives
1 cup heavy cream

This is one of the best ways to utilize leeks.

1. In a soup pot, melt the butter. Add the onions and sauté until golden brown, about 10 minutes. Mix in the salt, pepper, and nutmeg. Add the leeks and celery and cook for 15–20 minutes, adding a little of the water to keep the vegetables from sticking.
2. Add the potatoes, cover, and continue to cook, stirring occasionally and gradually adding the remaining water until the potatoes are done.
3. Add the milk and chives, and simmer gently for 15 minutes to blend the flavors.
4. Just before serving, mix in the heavy cream and heat to simmering. Taste and reseason.

MUSHROOM POTATO LEEK SOUP
Slice about 1/2 pound of mushrooms and sauté them in the butter before you add the onions.

COLD VICHYSSOISE
This is a classic summer soup. Blend the soup after adding the milk and the chives. Chill thoroughly. Swirl in the heavy cream. Taste and reseason.

Yield: Serves 6

Tomato Bisque

1 quart tomato juice
1 carrot, finely grated
3 celery stalks, finely chopped
4 scallions, finely chopped
2 tablespoons olive oil
1 onion, finely chopped
1 green pepper, finely chopped
2 cloves of garlic, finely chopped
1 teaspoon dried basil or 1 tablespoon
  finely chopped fresh basil
1/2 teaspoon dried marjoram or 2
  teaspoons finely chopped fresh marjoram
1/4–1/2 teaspoon black pepper
1 medium-size zucchini, finely chopped, or
  8–10 ounces fresh spinach, finely
  chopped
1 cup sour cream

This quick never-fail soup gets lots of compliments at the restaurant. It's thick with vegetables and smooth with sour cream.

1. In a soup pot, bring the tomato juice to a boil, then add the carrot, celery, and scallions. Reduce the heat and continue to simmer.
2. In a separate frying pan, heat the oil. Add the onion, green pepper, and garlic and sauté until limp. Add the herbs and pepper and sauté for about 1 minute. Add the zucchini or spinach and cook until tender.
3. Add the cooked vegetables to the tomato mixture. Simmer for 30 minutes.
4. Just before serving, remove 1–2 cups of the soup to a separate bowl. Mix thoroughly with the sour cream, then return to the rest of the soup.
5. Salt the soup to taste.

TOMATO VEGETABLE BISQUE
You can use any extra vegetables you like in this soup. Broccoli, cauliflower, and eggplant are very good instead of or in addition to the zucchini. Start sautéing them at the point you would add the zucchini in the recipe, and cook until tender.

Yield: Serves 6

Mushroom Barley Soup

1/2 cup uncooked barley

8 cups water

2 bay leaves

2 tablespoons olive oil

12 ounces mushrooms, sliced

1 carrot, thinly sliced

2 celery stalks, thinly sliced

1 cup fresh or frozen lima beans

1/2 teaspoon dried or finely chopped fresh thyme

1/2 teaspoon black pepper

1/4 cup tamari or soy sauce

1/4 cup finely chopped fresh chives or scallions

1/4 cup finely chopped fresh parsley

We inherited this classic soup recipe from the previous owners of Cabbagetown.

1. Measure the barley, water, and bay leaves into a soup pot. Bring to a boil, then reduce the heat and simmer, partially covered, stirring occasionally to keep the barley from sticking. Cook for about 1 hour, or until the barley is tender.

2. In a separate frying pan, heat the oil. Add the mushrooms and sauté over high heat searing them to get maximum flavor. Lower the heat and add the carrot, celery, and lima beans. Cook for 10–15 minutes, or until the vegetables are tender. Add the thyme and pepper, and cook for 2–3 minutes more.

3. Add the cooked vegetables to the soup pot, along with the tamari, chives or scallions, and parsley.

4. Continue to simmer for 30 minutes to blend the flavors. Taste and adjust the seasonings. This soup gets very thick. When you reheat it, add more water, then reseason it with tamari, pepper, and more chopped parsley to freshen it.

Yield: Serves 6

Chinese Mushroom Soup

1/4 cup olive oil
2 onions, cut in crescents
3 cloves of garlic, finely chopped
1 carrot, sliced
1 potato, diced
6 cups water
12 ounces mushrooms, whole or cut in half
1/4 cup tamari or soy sauce

This soup gets richer in flavor the longer you simmer it.

1. In a soup pot, heat the oil. Add the onions and garlic and sauté until just translucent.
2. Add the carrot and potato, and continue to sauté until lightly cooked.
3. Add the water and heat until simmering.
4. Add the mushrooms and continue to simmer for 1–2 hours, to deepen the flavors.
5. Add the tamari or soy sauce. Taste and reseason.

Yield: Serves 6

Greek Spinach Soup

1/2 cup uncooked brown rice
10 cups water (or combination water and
  olive juice)
2 bay leaves
1 teaspoon dried or fresh whole rosemary,
  slightly crushed in your hands
1 onion, finely chopped
1/4 cup olive oil
2 onions, finely chopped
6 cloves of garlic, finely chopped
2 teaspoons dried basil or 2 tablespoons
  finely chopped fresh basil
1 teaspoon dried marjoram or 1 tablespoon
  finely chopped fresh marjoram
1 teaspoon dried mint or 1 tablespoon
  finely chopped fresh mint
1 teaspoon freshly ground black pepper
1 cup chopped black olives
8–10 ounces fresh spinach or Swiss chard,
  finely chopped (6 cups)
1/2 teaspoon salt
1/4 cup finely chopped scallions
Juice of 1 lemon

This soup was invented one day when we came to work and found that a good friend had been hurt in a car accident. We cooked that day with great concentration to keep our emotions steady and invented 3 new recipes.

1. Measure the rice, water (or water and olive juice), bay leaves, rosemary, and 1 chopped onion into a soup pot. Bring to a boil, then reduce the heat and simmer, partially covered, until the rice is done, about 40 minutes.
2. In a separate frying pan, heat the oil. Add the 2 onions and garlic and sauté until translucent, about 3 minutes. Add the herbs and pepper and sauté for 2–3 minutes, stirring frequently. Add the olives and sauté for 2–3 minutes. Add part of the spinach. Wait for it to wilt, then add more. Continue in this fashion until all the spinach is in the pan and well-cooked. Add a little water if necessary to keep the spinach from sticking.
3. Add the cooked vegetables to the soup pot, along with the salt. Continue to simmer for at least 30 minutes to blend the flavors, stirring frequently.
4. About 10 minutes before serving, mix in the scallions and lemon juice. Cook for 10 minutes more, then taste and adjust the seasonings. You may want to add more freshly ground black pepper.

Yield: Serves 6

Eddy St. Onion Soup

VEGETABLE STOCK

1–2 potatoes, chopped (essential)
Any good vegetable scraps: onion skins, garlic cloves and peels, celery tops and leaves, mushooms, carrot peels and scraps, fresh herb stems. Do not use peppers (which become bitter), or cabbage, broccoli, and cauliflower (which are too strongly flavored).
A few bay leaves
12 black peppercorns
2 tablespoons butter

SOUP

3 tablespoons butter
6–8 pounds onions, cut in crescents
4 cloves of garlic, finely chopped
1/2 teaspoon mustard powder
1/2 teaspoon dried or finely chopped fresh thyme
1/4 cup tamari or soy sauce
1/2 cup sherry
1/4 cup finely chopped fresh parsley
Salt and pepper to taste

This vegetarian version of the classic French Onion Soup depends on a strong, flavorful vegetable stock.

1. Make the stock. Fill a large pot about halfway with loosely packed vegetable scraps and the seasonings. Add water until the pot is 2/3–3/4 full. Bring to a low boil, then reduce the heat and simmer for 1–2 hours. Pour through a strainer.
2. In a large soup pot, melt 3 tablespoons butter. Add sliced onions and garlic. Over medium heat cook the onions down for 45–60 minutes or until the onions begin to brown and caramelize. Add small amounts of water to prevent scorching.
3. Add the mustard and thyme, and cook for 2–3 minutes.
4. Add the stock until you reach a good serving consistency. Add the tamari, sherry, and parsley. Continue simmering for at least an hour to deepen the flavors.
5. Add more stock if necessary. Add salt and pepper to taste.
6. Serve the soup just as it is or serve it the French way: In each bowl of soup, float 3 or 4 whole wheat croutons that have been sautéed in butter and garlic. Cover with grated cheese—a good Swiss, Gruyère, or Parmesan—or a sprinkle of bleu cheese. Pop under a broiler or heat in the oven to melt the cheese. Serve piping hot.

Yield: Serves 6

Cold Gazpacho

1 onion
1 cucumber, peeled
1 green pepper
2 cloves of garlic, finely chopped
6–8 fresh ripe tomatoes or 1 quart canned
   tomatoes
Juice of 1 lime or 1 tablespoon red wine
   vinegar
1 tablespoon good olive oil (The better the
   oil, the better the soup; if you don't have
   a good oil, leave it out.)
1/2 teaspoon salt
1/4 teaspoon black pepper

Here you have the number 1 cold soup. This is the summertime favorite at Cabbagetown. The recipe can be made with fresh or canned tomatoes, chopped by hand or in a blender or food processor. *But*, here are our ratings of gazpacho:

    1. Best! hand-chopped with fresh tomatoes.
    2. Hand-chopped, with canned tomatoes.
    3. Blended with fresh tomatoes.
    4. Blended with canned tomatoes.

1. Chop all the vegetables as finely as your patience allows. Or combine all the vegetables, coarsely chopped, in the blender or food processor. Blend for a short time, then continue pulsing the machine on and off to get a nice, evenly chunked soup.
2. Mix in the seasonings.
3. Chill thoroughly. Taste.

THE GAZPACHO BAR
Start with a big bowl of finely chopped tomatoes, chilled. Surround it with bowls of the other gazpacho vegetables, and bowls of chopped black olives, chopped hard-boiled eggs, chopped radishes, chopped scallions. Let each person assemble his or her own soup. Serve with crusty bread and butter.

Yield: Serves 6

Chilled Blender Borscht

1 pound beets
2 bay leaves
2 tablespoons butter
2 onions, chopped
1 carrot, chopped
1 wedge cabbage, chopped (4 cups)
Beet greens, chopped (optional)
2 teaspoons caraway seeds
1 teaspoon dried dill weed or 1 tablespoon
  finely chopped fresh dill
Juice of 2 lemons
1/2 teaspoon salt
1/4 teaspoon black pepper
Sour cream
Finely chopped fresh chives or scallions
  (optional)

This is the classic bright purple beet soup.

1. Scrub the beets thoroughly. Cook with bay leaves in water to cover for about 45 minutes, or until tender. Remove the bay leaves.
2. In a soup pot, melt the butter. Add the onions, carrot, cabbage, beet greens, caraway seeds, and dill and sauté until all the vegetables are very tender.
3. If the beet skins are tough, slip them off. If not, leave them on. Blend the cooked beets, beet water, and vegetables, adding more water if necessary to reach a good consistency.
4. Add the lemon juice, salt, and pepper.
5. Chill thoroughly. Taste and reseason.
6. Serve with a dollop of sour cream on each bowl of soup. Sprinkle with finely chopped chives or scallions for brilliant contrast.

Yield: Serves 6

Cold Bulgarian Cucumber Walnut Soup

2 cucumbers, peeled and diced
1 cup chopped walnuts
1 tablespoon good olive oil
1/2 cup finely chopped fresh dill (Do not make this with dried dill.)
4 cups yoghurt
1 cup sour cream
2 cups half-and-half

A customer left her copy of this recipe on a table in the restaurant. We tried it right away and liked it. Customers comment, "We love the walnuts!"

1. Mix the cucumbers, walnuts, olive oil, and dill together. Cover and place in the refrigerator for 2 hours.
2. Add the yoghurt, sour cream, and half-and-half.
3. Chill thoroughly before serving.

Yield: Serves 6

Cold Carrot Orange Soup

2 tablespoons butter
1/4 cup almonds, coarsely chopped
2 onions, chopped
8 carrots, coarsely chopped (6 cups)
2 bay leaves
2 whole cloves
1-inch piece stick cinnamon
Juice of 4 oranges
1 cup heavy cream

I learned to make something like this in French cooking school.

1. In a soup pot, melt the butter. Add the almonds, onions, and carrots and sauté until the carrots start to become tender. Add water to cover, the bay leaves, cloves, and cinnamon stick. Simmer, partially covered, for about 15 minutes, or until the carrots are soft.
2. Allow the carrot mixture to cool. Remove the bay leaves, cloves, and cinnamon stick.
3. Blend the carrot mixture with the orange juice and cream. Dilute to a good serving consistency with more orange juice.
4. Chill thoroughly. Taste and reseason.

Yield: Serves 6

Cold Cantaloupe Yoghurt Soup

1 ripe cantaloupe
4 cups yoghurt
1/4 cup honey
Grated rind of 1 orange
Juice of 1 orange
1/4 teaspoon cinnamon
Fresh mint

This is a pretty, light, and fresh-tasting soup. The cantaloupe should be very ripe.

1. Peel and seed the cantaloupe. Blend the cantaloupe pulp with all the other ingredients in a blender or food processor.
2. Chill thoroughly. Taste and reseason.
3. Serve garnished with a sprig of mint.

COLD FRUIT SOUP
Try this soup with 4 cups of strawberries, red raspberries, or ripe peaches instead of the cantaloupe. Blend in a banana for extra richness.

Yield: Serves 6

Cold Cream of Summer Green Soup

8–10 ounces fresh spinach, or combination spinach and Swiss chard (6 cups chopped)
1 cup lightly packed fresh green herbs (parsley, chives, dill, mint)
4 cups buttermilk
1 cup sour cream
1/2 teaspoon salt
1/4 teaspoon cayenne
1 cucumber, peeled and finely diced
Lemon juice (optional)

This is about the quickest and easiest summer soup to make. It's cold, flavorful, and refreshing.

1. Combine all the ingredients, except the cucumber, in a blender or food processor and blend until smooth. Stir in the diced cucumber.
2. Chill thoroughly. Taste and reseason. You might want to add a little lemon juice.

Yield: Serves 6

Cold Cucumber Barley Soup

1/4 cup uncooked barley
2 onions, chopped
2 tablespoons dill seed
2 cups water
3 cucumbers, peeled and chopped
1 cup finely chopped watercress
Juice of 2 lemons
1/2 teaspoon salt
1 cup milk
2 cups yoghurt
Finely chopped fresh chives

This soup has a unique texture from the cooked and blended barley. It's the first cold soup I ever made at the restaurant.

1. Cook the barley, onions, and dill seed in the water, covered for about 1 hour, or until the barley is tender. Add the cucumbers and watercress and cook for 10 minutes. Cool the mixture.
2. Blend the cooled barley mixture with the lemon juice, salt, and milk until smooth. Mix in the yoghurt.
3. Chill. Taste and reseason.
4. Serve sprinkled with finely chopped chives.

Yield: Serves 6

Pasta & Pizza

If you want to stay alive in the restaurant business, you have to keep up with food trends. Pasta is definitely the trend of the 80s. You can cook up lemon basil fettuccine, artichoke linguine, or mixed spinach, tomato, and egg spirals, and top them with tomato sauce or pesto or garlic and olive oil. Then you can sit down with some good bread and wine and forget that anything could possibly go wrong with the world.

The other food of the 80s is pizza, especially delicious with our light whole wheat crust.

How to Cook Pasta

1 teaspoon dried basil
1/2 teaspoon dried whole rosemary,
   slightly crushed in your hands
2 tablespoons olive oil
1 pound pasta
2 tablespoons butter (Kevin recommends
   unsalted butter as having the best flavor.)
Fresh lemon juice

Kevin Anderson, who built the beautiful front door at Cabbagetown, showed us this method for cooking pasta. The pasta always has a good texture and extra flavor because of the added herbs. We use this method for all pasta—for salads, casseroles, tossed pasta dishes, and pasta with sauce. One pound of pasta serves 4 people.

1. Fill a soup pot or any large pot about 2/3 full of water. Add the basil and rosemary and bring to a boil.

2. Add the oil and the pasta. Return to a boil, stir once, and cover. Turn off the heat.

3. Leave the pasta until it is done *al dente*, usually 8–12 minutes for dried pasta, 3–4 minutes for fresh or frozen pasta. Stir once or twice to keep it from sticking to the bottom of the pot. The surest way to tell if pasta is done is to take out a piece and bite it. It's done when it's cooked through except for a tiny hard core right at the center.

4. Pour the pasta into a colander to drain it, but do not rinse. A bit of stickiness is part of the charm of pasta. Kevin says the Italians think Americans are crazy to rinse pasta.

5. Return the pasta to the cooking pot and toss in 2 tablespoons butter. The butter enriches the flavor and keeps the strands separate. Taste. Add a few squeezes of fresh lemon juice, and maybe a little salt until all the flavors are clear and distinct. The pasta is now ready to use.

Yield: Serves 4

Pasta with Garlic and Fresh Herbs

1 pound pasta
3 tablespoons olive oil
8–16 cloves of garlic, cut in thin slices
2 cups finely chopped fresh green herbs
1/2 teaspoon salt
Freshly ground black pepper
1–2 cups milk or heavy cream
Fresh lemon juice (optional)
Freshly grated Parmesan cheese

In the summer we use a mixture of fresh basil, chives, dill, parsley, and coriander leaves for this dish. In the winter when fewer fresh herbs are available we make it with parsley and scallions. Don't use dried herbs. They aren't the same. This is about my favorite Cabbagetown entrée to make at home. I love garlic! This is easy to make, fresh-tasting, and very satisfying.

1. Cook, drain, and season the pasta according to the instructions on page 109.
2. In a small frying pan, heat the olive oil. Add the garlic and sauté until very lightly browned. Remove from the heat.
3. Return the pot of cooked pasta to medium heat. Toss in the fried garlic, the herbs, salt, and pepper.
4. Add milk or cream slowly, cooking and tossing the pasta until the liquid is absorbed. When the milk or cream forms a little sauce around the pasta, you've added enough.
5. Taste. You might want to add a little fresh lemon juice, salt, or pepper to make all the flavors stand out. Serve with freshly grated Parmesan cheese and the pepper grinder on the table.

Yield: Serves 4

Pasta with Pesto

1 pound pasta
1 cup Jody's and Betsy's Presto Pesto
  (page 112)
1 cup milk or heavy cream
Juice of 1/2 lemon
Freshly ground black pepper
Freshly grated Parmesan cheese
2 fresh ripe tomatoes, chopped
About 1/2 cup Pesto

I think this is one of the great pasta dishes.

1. Cook, drain, and season the pasta according to the instructions on page 109.
2. Return the pot of cooked pasta to medium heat. Add 1 cup pesto and stir constantly while the pesto cooks into the pasta. Gradually add 1 cup milk or cream to form a little sauce.
3. Add the lemon juice, and freshly ground black pepper to taste.
4. On each individual plate serve a mound of the hot pasta. Sprinkle with Parmesan cheese, then with chopped fresh tomatoes. Put a dollop of pesto right in the middle. Eat immediately.

Yield: Serves 4

Jody and Betsy's Presto Pesto

1/2 cup pine nuts or walnuts
3 cloves of garlic
3/4 cup freshly grated Parmesan or
    Romano cheese or a combination of both
1/4 teaspoon salt
3 cups lightly packed fresh basil leaves
3/4 cup olive oil

Pesto is one of the major treats of the summer when fresh basil is abundant. You can store pesto in the refrigerator covered with a thin layer of olive oil or you can freeze it for special occasions in the winter.

1. Measure all the ingredients into a blender or food processor. Blend until smooth. I usually have to stop the machine a few times and push the mixture down into the blades with a wooden spoon.

2. Taste. Add more salt or freshly ground black pepper if you like. Presto! You now have pesto. Pesto is a good seasoning for pasta, rice, cooked potatoes, Mexican food, and steamed or stir-fried vegetables. Try it everywhere.

FRESH HERB PESTO
Substitute 1 cup of a different fresh green herb or mixture of green herbs for 1 cup of the basil. I like pestos made with parsley, chives, dill, or with a mixture of parsley and mint, thyme, or summer savory.

SPINACH PESTO
This has an excellent flavor. Substitute 3 cups fresh spinach leaves and 1 teaspoon dried basil for the fresh basil leaves. This pesto can be made year round.

Yield: 2 cups

Serving Pasta with a Sauce

After cooking, draining, and seasoning pasta according to the directions on page 109, cover the pot to keep the pasta hot. If it does cool down, add a little milk to prevent sticking, return to the heat, and reheat, stirring constantly.

Put the pasta in individual serving bowls or plates. Dot each serving with about 1 teaspoon butter. (Kevin recommends unsalted butter as having the best flavor.) Then cover the pasta with *just a little* sauce. Don't use too much sauce or you'll lose the flavor of the pasta. Sprinkle with freshly grated Parmesan or Romano cheese, and serve immediately. Put extra cheese and the pepper grinder on the table.

I was in California recently and found that at Chez Panisse, the trend-setting new cuisine restaurant, they shave Parmesan or Romano cheese rather than grating it. Use an ost hyvel (a Scandinavian cheese plane). Everything tastes lighter and fresher because of the air space between the food and the cheese.

The Simplest Tomato Sauce

3 tablespoons olive oil
1 onion, chopped
4 cloves of garlic, finely chopped
Freshly ground black pepper
1 teaspoon dried or finely chopped fresh
   oregano
1 quart canned tomatoes or 6–8 fresh ripe
   tomatoes, chopped
Salt to taste

When you have good pasta and want to show it off in style, this simple sauce is what you're looking for.

1. In a medium-size frying pan, heat the olive oil. Add the onion and garlic and sauté until tender, about 3 minutes. Add the pepper and oregano and cook 1 minute more, stirring constantly.

2. Add the canned or fresh tomatoes and simmer for about 15 minutes, until the sauce starts to thicken. Add salt to taste. Canned tomatoes usually have enough salt, but you might want to add 1/2–1 teaspoon salt to a fresh tomato sauce.

3. Keep the sauce warm until you're ready to serve it over freshly cooked pasta. Sprinkle generously with Parmesan cheese.

Yield: 2 1/2 cups. Serves 4–6

Kelly's Zucchini Sauce

2 medium-size zucchini (6 cups sliced)
6 tablespoons butter
Juice of 1/2 lemon
Pinch salt
3 carrots, julienne sliced and steamed

This sauce is quick, unusual, and delicious. Kelly, one of my recipe testers, wanted one of her own recipes in the book.

1. Slice the zucchini and steam or blanch it for about 6 minutes, or until it is soft.
2. In a blender, combine the zucchini with the butter, lemon juice, and salt. Blend until smooth. Taste and adjust the seasonings.
3. Return to the cooking pot and keep warm over low heat until ready to serve.
4. Serve over freshly cooked pasta, sprinkled with steamed julienne carrots. Do not serve this with Parmesan cheese, as the flavor is delicate and complete in itself.

Yield: Serves 4–6

Greg's Mushroom Stroganoff

1 1/2 pounds mushrooms
3/4 cup butter
6 tablespoons cream or dry sherry
Salt
Freshly ground black pepper
1 onion, finely chopped
1 cup sour cream
1/2 teaspoon paprika
Pinch cayenne
Pinch nutmeg
1 pound pasta

Greg was a regular customer—he downed Cashew Chili and a Genny Cream Ale 3 times a week, since it was "the cheapest way to get a good meal in town." He wanted to work at the restaurant, but we didn't have an opening. On a very busy Friday night, Greg was sitting at the long table eating his usual when Betsy broke a glass in the sink and cut her hand. While someone took care of Betsy, I looked frantically at the dishes piling up. With a flash of inspiration I rushed out to Greg and asked, "Do you *really* want to work here?" I pointed to the sink. Since then Greg has held down almost every job in the restaurant.

Greg learned to cook by doing a good portion of the recipe testing for this book. Mushroom Stroganoff is his favorite dish. The method is crucial: cook the mushrooms in small batches over high heat, and your stroganoff will be extraordinarily good.

1. Rinse the mushrooms thoroughly and cut in quarters. You will have about 6 cups of mushrooms.
2. Heat a medium-size frying pan over low heat. Add 2 tablespoons butter. When the butter is almost melted, add 1 cup mushrooms. Stir. Add 1 tablespoon sherry, a pinch of salt, and a grind of pepper. Stir and cook for 2–3 minutes, until the mushrooms are lightly browned and surrounded by a caramelized gravy. The mixture should be bubbly and sticky. If not, increase the heat and cook longer. Remove the mushrooms and gravy to a bowl. Melt another 2 tablespoons

butter and continue frying 1 cup batches of mushrooms with sherry, salt, and pepper until you have used all the mushrooms. By the time you are done there should be a fair amount of gravy, about 2/3 cup, in the bowl.

3. Put half the gravy, about 1/3 cup, in the frying pan. Add the finely chopped onion and simmer over medium heat for about 5 minutes, until the onion is sweet and soft.

4. While the onion is simmering, mix the remaining gravy with the sour cream, paprika, cayenne, and nutmeg in a medium-size pot. Mix in the cooked onions and the mushrooms. Simmer for 5 minutes over very low heat to blend the flavors. Stir frequently. Taste.

5. Cook, drain, and season the pasta according to the instructions on page 109.

6. To serve put the cooked pasta on individual dinner plates, dot with butter, cover with stroganoff, and serve immediately.

Yield: Serves 4–6

Sydell's Pasta with Eggplant

4–5 cups Simplest Tomato Sauce (double the recipe on page 114)
1 medium-size eggplant (1 1/2 pounds)
2 eggs
1/2 cup whole wheat bread or pastry flour
1/4 teaspoon salt
1/2 teaspoon black pepper
1/2 teaspoon dried or finely chopped fresh thyme
Light vegetable oil for frying
1/2–1 pound mozzarella cheese
1 pound spaghetti, linguine, or fettuccine
Freshly grated Parmesan cheese

This is a fancy version of eggplant parmigiane.

1. First prepare the tomato sauce.
2. Wash the eggplant, but don't peel. With a serrated bread knife, slice the eggplant *lengthwise* in slices 1/4–1/2 inch thick. The slices will be shaped like shoe soles and you will probably get 6–8 of them.
3. Beat the eggs in a shallow bowl. On a plate, mix the flour, salt, pepper, and thyme. Dip each eggplant slice on both sides first in the eggs, then in the flour mixture.
4. In a frying pan, heat 3 tablespoons oil. Add as many eggplant slices as will fit. Fry them for about 3 minutes on each side, or until lightly browned. Drain on paper towels or a brown paper bag. Add 2 tablespoons more oil to the pan and fry the next batch of eggplant. Continue until all are fried.
5. Slice the mozzarella so you have 1 slice of cheese for each slice of eggplant. Fold each eggplant in half over a slice of cheese. Arrange on a baking tray. The eggplant can be baked right away or stored in the refrigerator.
6. Before you want to serve it, bake the eggplant in a preheated 350°F. oven for 20–30 minutes, or until the eggplant is piping hot and the cheese is melted.
7. Meanwhile cook, drain, and season the pasta according to the directions on page 109.
8. Serve hot pasta on individual serving plates. Top with a little sauce, 1 or 2 slices of eggplant, more sauce, and grated Parmesan cheese.

Yield: Serves 4–6

Vegetable Lo Mein

SESAME GARLIC SAUCE

8 cloves of garlic, finely chopped

1-inch piece fresh ginger, finely chopped

1/2 cup peanut butter

4 teaspoons dark sesame oil

1/4 cup rice wine vinegar of juice of 1
   lemon

1/4 cup tamari or soy sauce

1/4 teaspoon cayenne

LO MEIN

1/2 pound whole wheat spaghetti

1 head broccoli, cut in bite-size pieces
   (6 cups)

1 head cauliflower, cut in bite-size pieces
   (4 cups)

2 tablespoons light vegetable oil

1 medium-size zucchini or yellow summer
   squash, cut in bite-size pieces (4 cups)

2 carrots, grated

1/4 cup finely chopped fresh chives or
   scallions

1 cup Tamari-Roasted Almonds (page 59)

This very flavorful dish is made with cooked pasta and vegetables tossed together with a garlic sauce. You can use any kind of pasta, but I like whole wheat spaghetti the best—it has a nice texture with the sauce. Any vegetables you have on hand are good here. These are just my suggestions.

1. First prepare the sauce. Mix together the garlic, ginger, peanut butter, sesame oil, vinegar, tamari, and cayenne. Set aside.

2. Cook the spaghetti according to the instructions on page 109.

3. To prepare the vegetables, steam or blanch the broccoli and cauliflower for about 5 minutes, until just tender. Heat the oil in a medium-size frying pan and sauté the zucchini lightly. Mix the cooked vegetables all together with the grated carrots.

4. In a large pasta cooking pot, mix together the vegetables, scallions, cooked pasta, and sauce. Heat for about 3–4 minutes, until it's piping hot. Taste.

5. Serve sprinkled with almonds.

Yield: Serves 4

Mom's Macaroni and Cheese

3/4 cup uncooked whole wheat macaroni
3/4 cup soft bread crumbs (fresh or slightly
    stale bread, crumbled)
2 tablespoons butter
1/2 pound Cheddar cheese, grated (about 2
    cups)
1 1/4 cups hot milk
1 small onion, finely chopped
1/4 cup finely chopped fresh parsley
1/2 teaspoon salt
Sharp mustard (optional)
2 eggs, beaten
Paprika

Since I became a vegetarian, my mother has cooked this for me specially. It's very tender and custardy.

1. Cook the macaroni according to the instructions on page 109.
2. In a large bowl, combine the bread crumbs, butter, and cheese. Pour in the hot milk. Add the onion, parsley, and salt. At this point, taste. If the sauce is not flavorful or cheesy enough, add whatever you feel is lacking. You might want to add some sharp mustard.
3. Add the beaten eggs, then the cooked macaroni.
4. Pour into a well-buttered medium-size baking dish. Sprinkle with paprika.
5. Bake in a preheated 350°F. oven for about 30 minutes, until the casserole is firm and golden brown.
6. For best flavor, allow to sit for 10 minutes before serving.

Yield: Serves 2 hungry people or 4 not-so-hungry ones

Cabbagetown Lasagne Sauce

2 quarts canned tomatoes or 12–14 fresh
    ripe tomatoes, chopped
2 bay leaves
2 onions, diced
6–8 cloves of garlic, finely chopped
1 1/2 teaspoons fennel seeds
2 teaspoons dried basil or 2 tablespoons
    finely chopped fresh basil
1 teaspoon dried or finely chopped fresh
    oregano
2 teaspoons dried or finely chopped fresh
    thyme
1 teaspoon dried or fresh whole rosemary,
    slightly crushed in your hands
Freshly ground black pepper
Salt to taste

This flavorful sauce has the right juiciness for
our no-boil lasagne method.

1. In a large pot, cook the tomatoes with the
bay leaves, onions, and garlic. Simmer gently,
uncovered for about 1 hour, stirring frequently
to keep the tomatoes from sticking.
2. Add the herbs and pepper. Continue to
simmer for 30 minutes to blend the flavors.
At the restaurant we call this "letting the
ingredients get to know each other."
3. Taste and reseason. Canned tomatoes
usually have enough salt, but if you're using
fresh tomatoes, you might want to add about
1 teaspoon salt. If the sauce is bitter, add
more thyme or more black pepper, both of
which help sweeten tomatoes.

Yield: 1 1/2–2 quarts. Enough for 1 batch
Spinach Lasagne

Spinach Lasagne

1 1/2–2 quarts Cabbagetown Lasagne
  Sauce (page 121)
2 tablespoons olive oil
8–10 ounces fresh spinach, finely chopped
  (6 cups)
1/2 teaspoon salt
Freshly ground black pepper
15–16 ounces ricotta cheese (about 2 cups)
1 egg
Pinch nutmeg
1 teaspoon finely chopped fresh mint
  (optional)
1/2–3/4 pound whole wheat lasagne
  noodles
1 pound mozzarella cheese, thinly sliced
2 cups freshly grated Parmesan, Romano,
  or sharp Provolone cheese

This has been a favorite entrée at Cabbagetown from the day we opened the doors. A few employees have threatened to quit if I ever took it off the menu. Our lasagne technique has evolved through the years. Our most revolutionary discovery is that you don't have to cook the noodles before assembling the lasagne. If you cover the casserole and bake the noodles right in it, the lasagne is firmer and more flavorful. It's also much easier and less messy to make. Lasagne is a great company dish, since the flavors and textures are actually better if you make it in advance and heat it just before serving.

1. First prepare the sauce.
2. To make the filling, heat the oil in a medium-size frying pan. Add the spinach and sauté until lightly cooked. Season with salt and pepper. In a mixing bowl, combine the ricotta with the egg, nutmeg, and mint. Add the spinach and mix well.
3. Assemble the lasagne in a medium-size (3 quart or larger) baking dish. First, spread olive oil over the bottom of the dish to keep the casserole from sticking. Cover with a thin layer of lasagne sauce. Arrange a single layer of uncooked lasagne noodles over the sauce. Cover with half the ricotta mixture. Smooth it out. Cover with half the sliced mozzarella. Pat it down. Sprinkle with Parmesan cheese. Cover with another layer of sauce. Repeat the layers of noodles, the remaining ricotta mixture, the remaining mozzarella, and more Parmesan. Spread with another layer of sauce.

Cover with a final layer of noodles. Use the remaining sauce as a thick layer on top.
4. Cover the casserole dish. Do not use aluminum foil, since the tomato sauce will eat through it. Bake in a preheated 350 degrees F. oven for 1 hour to cook the noodles. Then sprinkle with more Parmesan cheese. Cover and return to the oven and bake 15–20 minutes. Turn off the heat and allow the lasagne to sit in the oven for 30–60 minutes to firm the textures and let the flavors ripen. Delicious!
5. Serve with a big salad and good red wine.

EGGPLANT PARMIGIANE LASAGNE

Slice 1 eggplant in thin slices. Dredge each slice with a coating of whole wheat flour, crushed rosemary, salt, and freshly ground black pepper. Fry the slices in olive oil. Put eggplant layers somewhere in the middle of the lasagne, and bake as directed above.

Yield: Serves 6–8

Pizza Crusts

1 1/2 cups hot water
2 tablespoons honey
1 tablespoon active dry yeast
2 1/2–3 cups whole wheat bread flour

This recipe makes three 9-inch pizza crusts (home-size pizzas baked in pie pans) or two 12-inch pizza crusts (the small pizzas you would find in a pizza place).

1. In a medium-size bowl, dissolve the honey in the water, stirring with a wooden spoon. Drop in the yeast while the water is still warm. When the yeast bubbles up, stir in enough flour to make a sticky dough. Turn onto a floured counter and knead until smooth and satiny, about 3 minutes.
2. Lightly oil the bowl, and return the dough to it. Turn the dough over so all of it is oiled. Allow to rise in a warm spot for about 60 minutes.
3. Oil the pizza pans lightly. Divide the dough into 2 or 3 balls, depending on what size pans you are using. Knead each ball separately. Then, using a rolling pin, roll each ball into a round to fit the pan. Pat the dough firmly into the pans.
4. Allow to rise in a warm spot for about 30 minutes.
5. The crusts are now ready for the toppings of your choice.

Yield: Three 9-inch crusts or two 12-inch crusts

Lisa and Craig arm wrestling after closing

Cabbagetown Cheese Pizza

**One 9-inch or 12-inch Pizza Crust
(page 124)**

**3/4 cup (for a 9-inch pizza) or 1 1/2 cups
(for a 12-inch pizza) Simplest Tomato
Sauce (page 114)**

**1 cup (for a 9-inch pizza) or 2 cups (for a
12-inch pizza) grated mozzarella cheese**

At Cabbagetown you can order plain cheese pizza with Italian tomato sauce or Mexican pizza with salsa. Each week we offer different vegetables as toppings. And chopped fresh garlic is gratis on any pizza. Here's how to make the plain cheese pizza.

1. First prepare the crusts and allow them to rise. Make the tomato sauce.
2. Cover the crust with tomato sauce and sprinkle on the cheese.
3. Bake in a preheated 425°F. oven for 25–30 minutes, until the cheese is well-melted and bubbly and the crust is firm and lightly browned.
4. Let the pizzas sit for about 5 minutes to settle. Then slice and serve. Have freshly grated Parmesan cheese, dried oregano, and cayenne or other hot pepper on the table.

Yield: One 9-inch pizza serves 1–2. One 12-inch pizza serves 2–4

MEXICAN PIZZA

Use Cooked Salsa (page 149) as the sauce and substitute grated Cheddar or Monterey Jack cheese for the mozzarella.

GREEK PIZZA

Sprinkle crumbled feta cheese and chopped black olives over the tomato sauce. Cover with mozzarella and bake.

TOFU PIZZA

Sprinkle small cubes of Marinated Tofu (page 54) over the tomato sauce. Cover with mozzarella and bake.

RICOTTA PIZZA

Spread the tomato sauce generously with ricotta cheese. Sprinkle with chopped fresh mint. Cover with mozzarella and bake.

PESTO PIZZA

Spread the pizza crusts with Jody's and Betsy's Presto Pesto (page 112). Sprinkle with chopped fresh tomatoes and chopped black olives. Cover with mozzarella and bake.

SPECIAL VEGETABLE PIZZAS

Sprinkle any of the following vegetables, or combination of them, over the tomato sauce. Cover with mozzarella and bake.

Fresh garlic, chopped
Red or white onions, thinly sliced
Green or sweet red peppers, sliced
Mushrooms, thinly sliced
Zucchini, sliced and lightly sautéed in olive oil
Eggplant, sliced and lightly sautéed in olive oil
Spinach, chopped, lightly sautéed in olive oil
Broccoli, steamed
Cauliflower, steamed
Asparagus, steamed
Green beans, steamed
Avocados, sliced
Green or black olives, chopped

Giselle's Father's E-Z A to Z Pizza

Two 9-inch Pizza Crusts or one 12-inch
  Pizza Crust (page 124)
2 tablespoons olive oil
6 ounces mushrooms, sliced (2 cups)
1/2 teaspoon freshly ground black pepper
2 tablespoons olive oil
1 onion, chopped
2 cloves of garlic, finely chopped
1 small zucchini, sliced (2–3 cups)
1 teaspoon dried basil or 1 tablespoon
  finely chopped fresh basil
1/2 teaspoon dried or finely chopped fresh
  oregano
1 ripe avocado, cut in cubes
2 eggs
1/2 pound mozzarella cheese, grated
  (2 cups)
1/4 teaspoon salt
3 tablespoons prepared French mustard
1 teaspoon sesame seeds (optional)

This pizza is made with egg custard instead of tomato sauce.

1. First roll out the crusts and allow to rise. Bake in a preheated 350°F. oven for about 25–30 minutes, until the crusts are firm and lightly brown.
2. In a medium-size frying pan, heat 2 tablespoons olive oil. Add the mushrooms and sauté over high heat until the mushrooms are lightly browned and succulent, about 5 minutes. Grind in the black pepper. Remove to a bowl.
3. Heat another 2 tablespoons olive oil in the same skillet. Add the onion, garlic, and zucchini. Sauté until the zucchini is tender, about 6 minutes. Add the herbs and sauté 1 minute more, stirring constantly. Turn off the heat and stir in the avocado and mushrooms.
4. In the bowl, beat the eggs. Mix in the grated cheese, salt, and vegetables.
5. Spread the pizza crust or crusts with mustard. Pop into a preheated 350°F. oven for about 5 minutes so the mustard flavor permeates the crusts.
6. Remove the crusts from the oven. Spread with the egg and vegetable mixture, and pop back into the oven for about 20–25 minutes, or until the pizza looks firm and lightly browned.
7. Sprinkle with sesame seeds. Let the pizzas stand for 5–10 minutes before serving.

Yield: Two 9-inch pizzas or one 12-inch pizza.
Serves 4

Quiches
Stir-Fries
Tofu Burgers &
the C-Town Slice

This chapter is a collection of the entrées that don't fit in any other chapter. But don't be deceived. These are actually the dishes I make most frequently at home. A quiche is often the most straightforward option for a medium-classy meal, and you can make a quiche very quickly if you have a pie crust frozen and ready. Stir-fries are a staple dinner in every vegetarian household. Our Herbed Rice recipe is included here. Tofu Burgers and the C-Town Slice are big sandwich meals—informal, but definitely good and filling.

Jill doing "front counter"

Whole Wheat Pie Crusts

2 1/2 cups whole wheat pastry flour
1/2 teaspoon salt (only if you are using
   unsalted butter)
3/4 cup cold butter
About 1/2 cup cold water or milk

These are for quiches and pies. They are very tender but you must use whole wheat *pastry* flour. Don't try making these with bread flour. The Cabbagetown trick for making quick pie crusts is to use cold butter and grate it into the flour. We always make 2 crusts at a time. If it's worth making 1, it's worth making 2. You can store the extra crust in a plastic bag in the freezer, and it's ready for an instant quiche or fruit pie.

1. In a mixing bowl, mix together the flour and salt (if you are using it) with a fork. Grate the cold butter with a medium grater over the flour. Toss with a fork until the butter is evenly distributed.
2. Toss in cold water or milk a little at a time and stir lightly with the fork. The exact amount of liquid will vary with the properties of the flour you are using, the temperature of the butter, how hot and humid the weather is, and the way you like your dough to feel when you roll it out. You have added enough liquid when you can press the dough with your hands and it holds together. The mixture will still look pretty loose and dry. It should not be wet or sticky.
3. Form the dough into 2 balls.
4. Butter two 9-inch or 10-inch pie pans well to prevent sticking.
5. Now roll out the crusts, 1 at a time. First knead the ball about 10 times on a floured counter so the ball holds together. To get it into the best shape for rolling, first press the dough down so it becomes a flattened ball. Then push it down in the center to make a

medium-size dent. Last, turn the dough around on the counter, pressing the edges with cupped palms so the whole edge becomes smooth.

6. Lift up the dough and lightly flour the whole counter. With a lightly floured rolling pin, roll the dough, starting from the center and rolling out. Turn the dough over frequently as you roll so it doesn't stick. Coutinue flouring the rolling pin and counter as needed.

7. Roll the crust until it shows about 1 inch around the top on an inverted pie pan. Fold the crust in half, and lift it into the pan. Unfold it, and ease it down so it fits smoothly. Fold under the edges of the crust, then flute the rim. If you haven't fluted a crust before, ask a friend to show you. It's satisfying to do and beautiful to look at.

8. Prick the crust with a fork and store it in a plastic bag in the refrigerator for a short time or the freezer for a longer time, until you're ready to use it.

Yield: Two 9-inch or 10-inch pie crusts

Quiche du Jour

One 9-inch or 10-inch Whole Wheat Pie
Crust (page 132)
3 tablespoons butter
1 onion, cut in crescents
2 cups chopped vegetables
Herbs (I especially like thyme, tarragon,
and dill.)
Black pepper
3 eggs
1/4 teaspoon salt
1 1/2 cups combination milk and heavy
cream (The more cream you use, the
richer your quiche will be.)
Pinch nutmeg or mustard powder
2 cups grated cheese or mixture of cheeses

Here is a basic recipe for quiche. Variations are on the following pages.

1. First roll out the pie crust.
2. Prepare the vegetables. In a medium-size frying pan, melt the butter. Add the onion and sauté for 2–3 minutes, until it just starts to get limp. Then add the vegetables you're featuring in the quiche and cook until quite tender. (You want the vegetables in a quiche to be well-cooked to bring out the deep and rich aspects of their flavor.) Add herbs and freshly ground black pepper to taste.
3. Next make the custard. In a medium-size bowl, beat the eggs with a whisk. Whisk in the salt, then the milk and heavy cream, then the nutmeg or mustard.
4. To assemble the quiche, sprinkle half the cheese in the the pie crust. Spread the vegetables over the cheese. Do not pack the vegetables tightly. The custard should get inside the vegetable layer and puff it up to make a light and delicate quiche. Sprinkle with the remaining cheese. Pour in as much custard as your pie crust will hold. If you have any custard left over, store it in the refrigerator. It will keep well for 2 days, and you can use it in an omelette or scrambled eggs or another quiche.
5. Bake in a preheated 350°F. oven for about 40 minutes, or until the quiche is lightly browned and the custard is firm in the center.
6. Allow to settle for 20 minutes before serving so the texture can firm and the quiche can cool to its best flavor.

Yield: One 9 or 10-inch quiche. Serves 4–6

Blushing Tomato Quiche

One 9-inch or 10-inch Whole Wheat Pie
   Crust (page 132)
3 tablespoons butter
1 onion, cut in crescents
3 fresh ripe tomatoes, cut in crescents
1/2 teaspoon dried or fresh whole
   rosemary, slightly crushed in your hands
1/2 teaspoon dried or finely chopped fresh
   thyme
1/4 teaspoon dried or finely chopped fresh
   tarragon
1 teaspoon dried dill weed or 2 tablespoons
   finely chopped fresh dill
2 tablespoons chopped capers or black
   olives
Freshly ground black pepper
3 eggs
1/4 teaspoon salt
1 1/2 cups combination milk and heavy
   cream
Pinch mustard powder
2 cups grated Swiss cheese

This is a fresh tomato quiche with capers or
black olives for a special touch.

1. First roll out the pie crust.
2. In a medium-size frying pan, melt the
butter. Add the onion and sauté for 2–3
minutes, until limp.
3. Add the tomatoes and herbs, and sauté for
about 5 minutes, until the tomatoes just start
to juice up and become tender. Add the
capers or black olives. Grind in black pepper
to taste.
4. Beat the eggs with a whisk in a medium-
size mixing bowl. Whisk in the salt, then the
milk and heavy cream, then the mustard.
5. Sprinkle half the cheese in the crust. Add
the tomato mixture, then the remaining
cheese. Pour in the custard. Bake in a
preheated 350°F. oven for about 40 minutes,
or until the quiche is lightly browned and the
custard is firm in the center.
6. Allow to settle for 20 minutes before
serving so the texture can firm and the quiche
can cool to its best flavor.

Yield: One 9 or 10-inch quiche. Serves 4–6

Zucchini Mushroom Quiche

One 9-inch or 10-inch Whole Wheat Pie
   Crust (page 132)
2 tablespoons butter
6 ounces mushrooms, sliced (2 cups)
Freshly ground black pepper
2 tablespoons butter
1 small zucchini, cut in bite-size pieces
   (1 1/2 cups)
2 tablespoons finely chopped fresh chives
   or scallions
3 eggs
1/4 teaspoon salt
1 1/2 cups combination milk and heavy
   cream
Pinch nutmeg or mustard powder
2 cups grated Swiss cheese

1. First roll out the pie crust.
2. In a medium-size frying pan, melt 2 tablespoons butter. Add the mushrooms and sauté over high heat for about 5 minutes, until the mushrooms are lightly browned and smell fragrant. Grind in a little black pepper. Remove to a bowl.
3. Melt the remaining 2 tablespoons butter in the same frying pan. Add the zucchini and sauté over medium heat for about 5 minutes, or until the zucchini is tender. Return the mushrooms to the frying pan and add the chives or scallions. Continue to sauté for 1–2 minutes to blend the flavors.
4. Beat the eggs with a whisk in a medium-size bowl. Whisk in the salt, then the milk and cream, then the nutmeg or mustard.
5. Sprinkle half the cheese in the crust. Add the vegetable mixture, then the remaining cheese. Pour in the custard. Bake in a preheated 350°F. oven for about 40 minutes, or until the quiche is lightly browned and the custard is firm in the center.
6. Allow to settle for 20 minutes before serving so the texture can firm and the quiche can cool to its best flavor.

HARVEST MUSHROOM QUICHE
Substitute 1 1/2 cups of peeled, thinly sliced winter squash (acorn or butternut) for the zucchini. Season with 2 tablespoons sherry while you are sautéing it.

Yield: One 9 or 10-inch quiche. Serves 4–6

Potato Sour Cream Quiche

One 9-inch or 10-inch Whole Wheat Pie Crust (page 132)
3 potatoes
3 tablespoons butter
1 onion, cut in crescents
1 teaspoon dried dill weed or 1 tablespoon finely chopped fresh dill
2 tablespoons finely chopped fresh parsley
2 tablespoons finely chopped fresh chives or scallions
3 eggs
1/4 teaspoon salt
1 1/4 cups combination milk and heavy cream
1/2 cup sour cream
Pinch nutmeg
2 cups grated Cheddar cheese

Potatoes are very good in a quiche.

1. First roll out the pie crust.
2. Scrub the potatoes well but do not peel. Cook in water to cover until the potatoes are tender but still firm, about 30 minutes after the water boils. Dice into small cubes.
3. In a medium-size frying pan, melt the butter. Add the onion and sauté for 2–3 minutes, until it just starts to get limp. Add the cooked potatoes and continue to cook over medium heat for about 5 minutes to blend the flavors. Stir frequently and add a little potato water if it starts to stick. Stir in the herbs and remove from the heat.
4. Beat the eggs with a whisk in a medium-size bowl. Whisk in the salt, then the milk and cream, then the sour cream, then the nutmeg.
5. Sprinkle half the cheese in the crust. Add the potato mixture, then sprinkle with the remaining cheese. Pour in the custard. Bake in a preheated 350°F. oven for 40 minutes, or until the quiche is lightly browned and the custard is firm in the center.
6. Allow to settle for 20 minutes before serving so the texture can firm and the quiche can cool to its best flavor.

Yield: One 9 or 10-inch quiche. Serves 4–6

Spinach Feta Quiche

One 9-inch or 10-inch Whole Wheat Pie
   Crust (page 132)
3 tablespoons olive oil
1 onion, cut in crescents
4 cloves of garlic, finely chopped
1 teaspoon dried basil or 2 teaspoons finely
   chopped fresh basil
1/2 teaspoon dried or finely chopped fresh
   thyme
5–6 ounces fresh spinach, chopped (4 cups)
1/4 cup chopped black olives
Freshly ground black pepper
3 eggs
1/4 teaspoon salt
1 1/2 cups combination milk and heavy
   cream
Pinch mustard powder
2 cups grated Swiss cheese
1/2 cup crumbled feta cheese

1. First roll out the pie crust.
2. In a medium-size frying pan, heat the oil. Add the onion and garlic and sauté for 2–3 minutes, until the onion is translucent. Add the basil and thyme and cook for 1 minute. Add the chopped spinach and cook until it is wilted. Add the olives and grind in black pepper to taste.
3. Beat the eggs with a whisk in a medium-size bowl. Whisk in the salt, then the milk and heavy cream, then the mustard.
4. Sprinkle half the Swiss cheese in the crust. Add the spinach mixture, then sprinkle on the feta, then the remaining Swiss cheese. Pour in the custard. Bake in a preheated 350°F. oven for 40 minutes, or until the quiche is lightly browned and the custard is firm in the center.
5. Allow to settle for 20 minutes before serving so the texture can firm and the quiche can cool to its best flavor.

Yield: One 9 or 10-inch quiche. Serves 4–6

Broccoli Bleu Cheese Quiche

One 9-inch or 10-inch Whole Wheat Pie
   Crust (page 132)
1 stalk broccoli, cut in bite-size pieces
   (2 cups)
3 tablespoons butter
1 onion, cut in crescents
1/2 teaspoon dried or fresh whole
   rosemary, slightly crushed in your hands
1/2 teaspoon dried or finely chopped fresh
   thyme
1/4 teaspoon dried or finely chopped fresh
   tarragon
Freshly ground black pepper
3 eggs
1/4 teaspoon salt
1 1/2 cups combination milk and heavy
   cream
Pinch mustard powder
2 cups grated Cheddar cheese
1/2 cup crumbled bleu cheese

The key to any broccoli quiche is to cook the broccoli until it's sweet and tender, but not overcooked. You do this by steaming it first, then sautéing it with onions.

1. First roll out the pie crust.
2. Steam or blanch the broccoli for about 5 minutes, until it's tender when you pierce it with a knife. Pour through a colander to drain.
3. In a medium-size frying pan, melt the butter. Add the onion and sauté for 2–3 minutes, until limp. Add the herbs, then the broccoli. Cook gently for about 2–3 minutes, until the flavors are well-blended. Grind in black pepper to taste.
4. Beat the eggs with a whisk in a medium-size bowl. Whisk in the salt, then the milk and heavy cream, then the mustard.
5. Sprinkle half the Cheddar cheese in the crust. Add the broccoli mixture, then sprinkle in the bleu cheese, then the remaining Cheddar. Pour in the custard. Bake in a preheated 350°F. oven for 40 minutes, or until the quiche is lightly browned and the custard is firm in the center.
6. Allow to settle for 20 minutes before serving so the texture can firm and the quiche can cool to its best flavor.

Yield: One 9 or 10-inch quiche. Serves 4–6

Dawn making a stir-fry

Herbed Rice

2 tablespoons light vegetable oil
2 onions, chopped
2 cloves of garlic, finely chopped
1 cup uncooked brown rice
2 1/2 cups water
2 teaspoons dried dill weed or 2
   tablespoons finely chopped fresh dill
1/2 teaspoon dried or finely chopped fresh
   thyme
1/2 teaspoon salt
1/2 teaspoon black pepper
1 tablespoon butter

This is our all-purpose rice. We sauté the dry rice with onions and garlic for a rich, toasty flavor, then cook it with herbs.

1. In a medium-size pot, heat the oil. Add the onions, garlic, and rice and sauté for 5 minutes, stirring frequently.
2. Add the water, herbs, salt, pepper, and butter. Stir so it is all mixed together.
3. Bring to a boil, then reduce the heat and simmer, covered for about 40 minutes or until the water is absorbed. Check the rice after 30 minutes. If there is a lot of water left, remove the cover and finish the cooking. Watch the rice so it doesn't stick. If the rice looks too dry, add a little more water. (Depending on age and variety, rice absorbs different amounts of water at varying speeds.)
4. Let the cooked rice sit in the pot, covered, for 15 minutes before serving. This allows the grains of rice to firm up so they stay separate and don't clump together.

Yield: 4 cups. Serves 4–6

Season's Stir-Fry

4 cups Herbed Rice (page 141)
2 cups Marinated Tofu (page 54)
2 stalks broccoli, cut in bite-size pieces
   (6 cups)
4 cloves of garlic, finely chopped
1/2-inch piece fresh ginger, finely chopped
2 tablespoons dark sesame oil
2 tablespoons light vegetable oil
2 carrots, sliced
2 celery stalks, sliced
2 onions, cut in crescents
1 green pepper, sliced
1 wedge green cabbage, coarsely sliced
   (2 cups)
2 tablespoons tamari or soy sauce
Rice wine vinegar or fresh lemon juice
   (optional)

The Cabbagetown stir-fry technique is really a combination of steaming and frying vegetables so they stay flavorful and crisp, but light rather than oily. We add tofu to the vegetables, season them with garlic, ginger, and tamari or soy sauce, and serve them over brown rice. A stir-fry is what you're looking for when you want a light, hot, and nutritious meal. You can vary it by using any vegetables that are in season.

From working in the restaurant kitchen I've developed a certain meticulousness in cooking, most obvious to me when I make stir-fries at home. I like to have the counter very clean, the vegetables very clean, and I like to put each vegetable in a separate little container as I cut it for the stir-fry. This is the way we do it in the restaurant. We're careful with the preparation, so when it comes time to cook the stir-fry, there is a feeling of order and care which makes cooking feel good.

1. First prepare the rice and the tofu.
2. Steam or blanch the broccoli for about 5 minutes until it's just tender when pierced with a knife. Pour it through a colander, saving the broccoli water for cooking the stir-fry. Rinse the broccoli with cold water to stop the cooking and set aside.
3. To prepare the seasoning mixture, chop the garlic and ginger together. Put it in a small bowl, and cover it with 2 tablespoons dark sesame oil.
4. It takes 15–20 minutes to cook a stir-fry, and you want to serve it immediately after you finish cooking it, so time your cooking

accordingly. When you are ready to begin (all the vegetables are ready), heat 2 tablespoons light vegetable oil in a large frying pan or wok. Toss in the carrots and cook for 2 minutes, stirring occasionally with a wooden spoon or wok spatula. Add 1/2 cup of broccoli water and steam-fry the carrots about 3 minutes more, or until most of the water is gone and the carrots are just starting to become tender. Add the celery and cook for about 3 minutes, until the celery just starts to become tender.

5. Add the onions, then the garlic-ginger-sesame oil mixture. Cook and stir until the onions just start to become limp, about 2 minutes. Add more broccoli water if necessary to keep the vegetables from sticking.

6. Add the broccoli and Marinated Tofu, and cook until warm, 2–3 minutes. Add more broccoli water if necessary.

7. Stir in the tamari or soy sauce, and immediately add the green peppers and cabbage. Stir well. Add 1–2 tablespoons more broccoli water, and continue cooking until the peppers and cabbage are hot, about 5 minutes. The mixture should look colorful and fresh, tender and juicy. That's the balance you're striving for. Taste. You might want to add a little rice wine vinegar or fresh lemon juice to sharpen the flavors.

8. Spoon 1 cup hot rice onto individual serving plates and top with a mound of hot vegetables. Chopsticks work better than forks with stir fries. Also put tamari or soy sauce and the pepper grinder on the table.

SPRING STIR-FRY
Steam asparagus instead of the broccoli. Add snow peas and fresh spinach leaves instead of the green pepper and cabbage.

SUMMER STIR-FRY
Steam green beans along with the broccoli. Add sliced zucchini instead of celery. Add finely chopped fresh green herbs to the seasoning mixture.

AUTUMN STIR-FRY
You can change the character of the sitr-fry by adding sliced fresh tomatoes. Add them right after the onions and cook so they juice up. Add fresh corn kernels after the tomatoes.

WINTER STIR-FRY
Slicc parsnips, potatoes, or sweet potatoes, and add them along with the carrots. Fry 2 cups sliced mushrooms separately in oil at high heat, until golden brown. Add along with the broccoli and tofu.

Yield: Serves 4

Tofu Burgers

3 tablespoons light vegetable oil
1 onion, diced
2 cloves of garlic, finely chopped
1 1/2 cups diced raw vegetables (I like
   celery, carrots, green peppers, and
   mushrooms)
1/2 cup chopped walnuts
2 teaspoons dried green herbs or 2
   tablespoons finely chopped fresh green
   herbs
1/2 teaspoon black pepper
1 1/2 cups crumbled tofu
2 eggs, beaten
1/2 cup soft bread crumbs
1/4 teaspoon salt
1/4 cup whole wheat bread or pastry flour
Light vegetable oil for frying
Cheddar cheese (optional)

This is a classic vegetarian item, filling the need for something hot and succulent to serve on a slice of bread.

1. In a medium-size frying pan, heat 3 tablespoons oil. Add the onion, garlic, raw vegetables, and walnuts and sauté until tender and lightly browned. Stir frequently to prevent sticking. Stir in the herbs and pepper, and cook for 1 minute more.
2. In a mixing bowl, combine the tofu, eggs, bread crumbs, and salt. Stir in the sautéed vegetable mixture.
3. Measure the whole wheat flour onto a plate. Form the tofu burger mixture into 6 patties. Dip each patty into the flour to cover it on both sides. The patties are fragile, so handle them with care.
4. Heat oil to cover the bottom of a frying pan. Fry each burger on one side until browned and crisp, about 5 minutes. Flip over and fry on the other side for 5 minutes.
5. Keep the burgers warm in the oven until serving. If you want cheese burgers, cover with Cheddar cheese to melt in the oven.
6. Serve each burger on a slice of whole wheat bread, toasted and buttered. Eat plain or topped with mustard, sautéed onion rings, salsa. To serve tofu burgers "Julie style," put each one on toasted, buttered whole wheat bread. Then mound a generous amount of green salad on top, and pour warmed Tarragon Vinaigrette Dressing (page 71) over it all. Crumbled bleu cheese on top is delicious.

TEMPEH BURGERS

Substitute 1/2 pound of tempeh for the tofu. Put the tempeh in a pot of boiling water to which you've added 1 tablespoon tamari or soy sauce. Return to a boil, then boil for 20 minutes. Put the tempeh in a colander to drain off the water, then crumble it. Proceed as with tofu burgers.

Yield: 6 tofu burgers. Serves 3 very hungry people or 6 people with normal appetites.

The C-town Special Sandwich

FOR 1 SANDWICH

1 slice homemade whole wheat bread
Butter
1–1 1/2 cups Cabbagetown Cole Slaw
(page 64)
2 tablespoons Rugged Garlic Dressing
(page 68)
Freshly ground black pepper
1 cup grated Swiss cheese
Salad greens

You can make these sandwiches 1 or 2 at a time in the toaster oven, or bake them on a cookie sheet in the oven.

1. For each sandwich, cut a slice of bread about 1/2 inch thick. Butter it and place it on a baking sheet.
2. Pile on as much cole slaw as you can fit, patting it down so it doesn't tumble. Then spoon 2 tablespoons dressing over the top. Cover with 1 cup grated Swiss cheese.
3. Bake in a preheated 350°F. oven or toaster oven for about 20 minutes, or until all the cheese is melted and bubbly around the edges.
4. Pry loose with a spatula, being sure to get all the delicious crusty cheese around the edges. Serve on individual serving plates on a bed of salad greens.

C-TOWN AVOCADO SLICE
Top the cole slaw with slices of ripe avocado.

C-TOWN VEGETABLE SLICE
Substitute a layer of sliced raw mushrooms or steamed broccoli for the cole slaw.

C-TOWN TOFU SLICE
Substitute a layer of Marinated Tofu (page 54) for the cole slaw. Serve it with extra Lemon Sesame Dressing (page 70) on the side.

Yield: Each sandwich serves 1 person

Mexican Entrées

Craig, our resident expert in Mexican cooking, says that Mexican spices are good for you. They perk you up. He drove across the country from California without touching coffee—he drank bottles of hot sauce instead. When he got to New York, he felt stimulated, alive, and healthy.

Before he came here, Craig lived in Santa Barbara and worked for the Social Security Department. Next door to his office was a little restaurant that served salsa and French bread with lunch. Craig and his co-workers loved the salsa so much that he tried making it at home—it is the salsa that Craig taught us to make at Cabbagetown.

When I asked him how he invented his refried beans recipe, he said, "Well, I found out what spices were involved in Mexican coooking—cumin, coriander, basil, etc.—and just started playing around with them until I got the exact flavor I wanted. I had to add dill, even though I'd never heard of it in Mexican food."

When I asked Craig what made Cabbagetown Mexican food special, he said, "We're willing to try almost anything. In Mexico they just don't eat vegetarian food. They have chicken or beef or lard in almost everything. So vegetarian Mexican food has to be something new."

The food we serve at Cabbagetown is milder than Craig or I like, but we have to cater to the tastes of upstate New Yorkers. "That trend is changing now," comments Craig. "There are more Mexican and Indian restaurants everywhere in the United States. People are getting used to spices and hot food. They are developing a tolerance for small amounts of pain. They're even starting to enjoy it!"

Cooked Salsa

1 quart canned tomatoes or 6 fresh ripe
  tomatoes
1 tablespoon ground cumin
1 teaspoon ground coriander
1/2 teaspoon cayenne
1/2 teaspoon dried or finely chopped fresh
  oregano
1/2 teaspoon dried basil or 2 teaspoons
  finely chopped fresh basil
3 tablespoons light vegetable oil
1 onion, finely chopped
4 cloves of garlic, finely chopped
1/2 teaspoon salt
2 green peppers, finely chopped

This is Craig's original salsa recipe. It's richly
flavored and mildly spicy. I recommend it as
the salsa for enchiladas and burritos. It's also
the best salsa to make if you're going to store
it. Because it's cooked, it keeps nicely for
about a week in the refrigerator, or for as
long as you like in the freezer.

1. Pour the tomatoes through a strainer or a
colander mounted in a bowl to drain off some
juice. You will need about 2 1/2 cups of
mostly drained tomatoes to make a thick
salsa. (save the juice to use in soup or in
refried beans.)
2. Finely chop the drained tomatoes or
squeeze them with your hands to make small
pieces. If you are using fresh tomatoes, chop
them up finely.
3. Measure out the spices and herbs and mix
them together so they're ready to use.
4. In a medium-size frying pan, heat the oil.
Add the onion and garlic and sauté for 3–4
minutes, so they just start to cook. Reduce the
heat and add the spice mixture. Sauté for 1
minute to enhance the flavors, stirring
constantly so nothing sticks and burns.
5. Add the tomatoes. Simmer canned
tomatoes for 5 minutes, fresh tomatoes for 15
minutes. Add the salt and green peppers and
simmer for 5 minutes more.
6. Taste and reseason. If you like hotter salsa,
add more cayenne.

Yield: 3 cups

Enchilada Del Día

2 cups Craig's Refried Beans (page 23)
  (optional)
2 cups Herbed Rice (page 141)
2 cups salsa (I recommend Cooked Salsa,
  (page 149)
2 cups enchilada filling (page 152–158)
2 tablespoons butter
4 corn tortillas
2–4 cups grated Monterey Jack or Cheddar
  cheese

This is our best selling entrée. We make a different enchilada filling every day, hence the "del dia." Fillings vary from simple classics like raw onions with fresh herbs and sour cream, to seasonal steamed asparagus with lemon and pepper, to our favorite spicy corn, green pepper, and almond filling. We roll the filling in soft-fried corn tortillas. We put one enchilada on an ovenproof dinner plate, surround it with herbed rice, top the enchilada with salsa, then sprinkle grated Cheddar or Monterey Jack cheese over it all. Then we bake each person's dinner right on the plate. If you don't have ovenproof plates, you can bake the enchiladas with salsa and cheese in a baking dish, keep the rice hot in a pot, and serve it all at once. I recommend that you serve refried beans with the rice on the plate with the enchiladas. (We don't do it in the restaurant because most of our customers don't eat the beans.)

1. Frist make the refried beans, herbed rice, and salsa.
2. Choose the enchilada filling you want from the recipes on the following pages. Prepare the filling.
3. In a medium-size frying pan, melt the butter. Soft-fry each corn tortilla in the butter by cooking it on one side until it starts to get limp, then turn it over and fry it for a second or two more until it's all soft. Roll 1/2 cup of filling inside each tortilla. Store the filled tortillas on a plate covered with a plastic bag in the refrigerator until you're ready to serve dinner.

4. On each ovenproof enchilada plate, put 1 rolled enchilada. Cover it with about 1/2 cup salsa, being especially careful to cover the ends of the enchilada so they don't dry out during baking. Arrange 1/2 cup herbed rice (and 1/2 cup refried beans) next to the enchilada on the plate. Sprinkle it all with 1 cup of grated cheese. Or put all 4 enchiladas in a baking dish, cover with salsa, and sprinkle with 2 cups of grated cheese.
5. Bake in a preheated 350°F. oven for 15–20 minutes, until the cheese is melted and bubbly around the edges.
6. Serve immediately. A dollop of sour cream or guacamole and a few black olives are excellent additions to each plate. I sometimes enjoy a very light cole slaw made with red cabbage and Tarragon Vinaigrette Dressing (page 71) as a side salad on enchilada plates.

Yield: 4 enchiladas. Serves 4

Adam's Enchilada Filling

1/2 cup almonds
3 tablespoons light vegetable oil
2 green peppers, diced
2 cups fresh or frozen corn
1 teaspoon ground cumin
1/2 teaspoon ground coriander
1/4 teaspoon cayenne
1 cup grated Cheddar cheese

Here is the original Cabbagetown enchilada. It's full of corn, green peppers, almonds, and cheese, and is very nicely spiced. Adam, who invented this enchilada, worked at Cabbagetown before my partner and I bought it, and stayed on as one of our chief moral supports.

1. Toast the almonds in a 350°F. oven or toaster oven for about 30 minutes, or until lightly browned. Chop in half.
2. Heat the oil in a frying pan. Add the green peppers and sauté over high heat until they are blistered and tender, about 3 minutes. Add the corn and cook for 2–3 minutes more. Add the spices and sauté for 1 minute, stirring constantly. Remove from the heat.
3. Mix in the almonds and Cheddar cheese. Taste.

Yield: 2 cups. Filling for 4 enchiladas.

Green Pea Cream Cheese Enchilada Filling

**8 ounces cream cheese, at room
  temperature**
2 cups fresh or frozen green peas

This is our instant enchilada.

1. If you are using fresh green peas, steam them briefly, for about 1–2 minutes. Rinse in cold water to stop them cooking. Use frozen green peas just as they come from the package.
2. In a mixing bowl, knead the cream cheese with your hand until it is soft. Mix in the green peas with your hand.

Yield: 2 cups. Filling for 4 enchiladas

Onion and Fresh-Herb Enchilada Filling

2 onions, diced
1/4 cup finely chopped fresh green herbs
   (I like parsley, chives, basil, dill, and
   fresh coriander leaves.)
1/2 cup sour cream
1/2 cup grated Cheddar cheese
Freshly ground black pepper

Mix together all the ingredients.

Yield: 2 cups. Filling for 4 enchiladas

Spinach Sour Cream Enchilada Filling

2 tablespoons butter
2 onions, diced
4 cloves of garlic, finely chopped
8–10 ounces fresh spinach, chopped
    (6 cups)
1/2 teaspoon dried basil or 2 teaspoons
    finely chopped fresh basil
1/2 teaspoon black pepper
1/4 teaspoon cayenne
1/2 cup grated Cheddar or Monterey Jack
    cheese
1/2 cup sour cream

1. In a medium-size frying pan, heat the butter. Add the onion, garlic, and spinach, and sauté until the spinach is completely wilted but still bright green. Mix in the basil, pepper, and cayenne.

2. Turn off the heat, and mix in the cheese and sour cream. Taste and adjust the seasonings if needed.

Yield: 2 cups. Filling for 4 enchiladas

Pepper Olive Enchilada Filling

3 tablespoons olive oil
2 green peppers, diced in 1-inch squares
1 teaspoon coriander seeds
8 ounces cream cheese, at room temperature
1/2 cup coarsely chopped black olives
Freshly ground black pepper
1/4 teaspoon cayenne
1/2 teaspoon ground coriander

This filling has intense, exciting flavors. The method is important.

1. Heat the oil in a medium-size frying pan. Add the green peppers and coriander seeds. Sauté over high heat for about 5 minutes, stirring frequently, until the peppers are blistered, lightly browned, and fragrant. Remove from the heat.
2. Mix in the cream cheese, black olives, and spices.

Yield: 2 cups. Filling for 4 enchiladas.

Mushroom Sour Cream Enchilada Filling

2 tablespoons butter
10 ounces mushrooms, sliced (3–4 cups)
1 onion, diced
4 cloves of garlic, finely chopped
1/4 teaspoon cayenne
1/2 teaspoon dried dill weed or 1
   tablespoon finely chopped fresh dill
1/2 cup sour cream

1. Heat the butter in a medium-size frying pan. Add the mushrooms, onion, and garlic and sauté for about 5 minutes, until the mushrooms are tender and most of the juice is cooked off. Mix in the cayenne and dill and cook for 1 minute more.
2. Turn off the heat and mix in the sour cream. Taste and adjust the seasonings.

Yield: 2 cups. Filling for 4 enchiladas

Asparagus Enchilada Filling

3 tablespoons butter
3 cups asparagus cut in bite-size pieces
2 cloves of garlic, finely chopped
1/4 teaspoon dried or finely chopped fresh tarragon
Freshly ground black pepper
Juice of 1/2 lemon
1 cup grated Cheddar or Monterey Jack cheese

1. Heat the butter in a medium-size frying pan. Add the asparagus and sauté until it is tender.
2. Add the garlic, tarragon, pepper, and lemon juice. Sauté for 1 minute more.
3. Turn off the heat and mix in the cheese. Taste and adjust the seasonings.

Yield: 2 cups. Filling for 4 enchiladas.

Burritos

2 cups Craig's Refried Beans
2 cups Cooked Salsa (page 149)
4 flour tortillas
2 cups grated Monterey Jack or Cheddar
 cheese
2 cups finely shredded lettuce or spinach
Sour cream or Guacamole (page 25)

A burrito is a flour tortilla that is filled, then rolled up. Our standard filling is refried beans. The variation that follows is for a spicy scrambled egg filling. When you're buying flour tortillas, check the list of ingredients carefully. Many commercial flour tortillas are made with lard. Natural foods stores often carry flour tortillas made without lard and with whole wheat flour instead of white flour. The refried beans have to be hot when you make burritos, but other than that burritos require no cooking.

1. First make the refried beans and salsa.
2. To assemble each burrito, sprinkle 1/2 cup grated cheese in a stripe down the center of a flour tortilla. Cover with a generous 1/2 cup of hot refried beans, and sprinkle with 1/2 cup of shredded lettuce or spinach. Roll the burrito up, and put it on a serving plate with the seam side down.
3. Top with 1/2 cup salsa and a big dollop of sour cream or guacamole. Serve immediately.

SCRAMBLED EGG BURRITOS
Instead of using refried beans, make up a scrambled egg filling. Beat 8 eggs with 1 finely diced green pepper, 1/2 teaspoon ground cumin, and 1/4 teaspoon cayenne. Heat 2 tablespoons butter in a frying pan and cook the egg mixture in the butter until it is well scrambled. Roll inside the flour tortillas with grated cheese and shredded lettuce.

Yield: Serves 4

Chile Rellenos

2 cups Craig's Refried Beans (page 23)
2 cups Herbed Rice (page 141)
2 cups Uncooked or Cooked Salsa (page 24)
   or (page 149)
4 medium-size hot peppers
1/2 pound Monterey Jack or mild Cheddar
   cheese
6 eggs, separated
4 tablespoons butter

The chile relleno we like the best, after all our experiments, is basically a puffy omelette with a cheese-filled hot pepper in the center. The most commonly grown hot peppers in New York State are Cubanelles and Hungarian hot wax peppers. Whichever pepper you use, you want it to be about 4 inches long and at least 1 inch wide. After you make the puffy omelettes, you bake them with salsa and cheese on top, and serve with rice and beans.

1. First make the refried beans, rice, and salsa.
2. To prepare the hot peppers, broil them on a tray under the broiler of your oven, turning them once, until they're browned and blistery all over. Put them inside a paper bag and allow them to steam for 10 minutes. Cut off the stems, pull off most of the thin outer skin, slit them about 2 inches down one side, and remove the seeds.
3. Slice part of the cheese into 4 finger-size pieces, and put 1 piece of cheese inside each hot pepper.
4. Beat the egg whites until stiff in a medium-size bowl. Beat the egg yolks until smooth in a separate bowl. Gradually fold the whites into the yolks, keeping the mixture as puffy as possible.
5. Melt 1 tablespoon of butter in a small frying pan or an omelette pan. Spoon some puffy egg batter about the size and shape of a stuffed hot pepper into the pan and allow it to cook for about 1 minute, until it is slightly firm. Lay a stuffed hot pepper gently in the batter, spoon some more batter over the top, and flip gently. Cook on the second side until

this little puffy omelette is slightly golden around the edges and firm. Put on an individual overproof serving plate or on a baking tray, whichever you will use to bake the rellenos.

6. Melt more butter in the pan and fry the remaining rellenos in a similar fashion. Keep stirring the eggs, since the yolks will separate out. Try to plan so you use all the batter.

7. Grate the remaining cheese.

8. If you are baking the rellenos on individual plates, cover each relleno with about 1/2 cup of salsa. Arrange 1/2 cup rice and 1/2 cup beans next to the relleno. Sprinkle it all with grated cheese. Or put all 4 rellenos in a baking dish, cover with salsa, and sprinkle with grated cheese.

9. Bake in a preheated 350°F. oven for 15–20 minutes, until the rellenos puff up and look luscious, and the cheese is melted and bubbly around the edge. Serve immediately.

Yield: Serves 4

Cashew Chili

1 1/2 cups uncooked pinto or kidney
    beans, sorted for stones and rinsed
6 cups water
2 bay leaves
2 tablespoons light vegetable oil
2 onions, chopped
4 cloves of garlic, finely chopped
2 green peppers, chopped
2 celery stalks, chopped
1 tablespoon butter
2 tablespoons ground cumin
1 tablespoon ground coriander
1/4 teaspoon cayenne
1/2 teaspoon dried or finely chopped fresh
    oregano
1/2 teaspoon dried basil or 2 teaspoons
    finely chopped fresh basil
1/2 teaspoon dried dill weed or 1
    tablespoon finely chopped fresh dill
1/2 teaspoon black pepper
2 teaspoons salt
1 quart canned tomatoes
1/2 cup cashews
2 teaspoons red wine vinegar

This spicy stew is a steaming feast in a bowl. It's almost the trademark of Cabbagetown.

1. Measure the beans, water, and bay leaves into a medium-size pot. Bring to a boil, then reduce the heat and simmer, partially covered, stirring occasionally to prevent sticking. Cook until the beans are tender, about 2 hours.
2. In a soup pot, heat the oil. Add the onions and garlic and sauté for about 2 minutes. Add the green peppers and celery, and cook until the vegetables are tender but still crisp, 8–10 minutes.
3. Melt in the butter, then add the spices, herbs, pepper, and salt. Sauté for 1–2 minutes, stirring frequently so nothing burns. (Cooking the spices takes the raw edge off their flavor.)
4. Add the tomatoes and tomato juice to the mixture, and crush the tomatoes with a wooden spoon. Simmer for 10 minutes, then remove from the heat until the beans are ready.
5. Toast the cashews in a 350°F. oven or toaster oven for 20 minutes, or until lightly browned. Be careful not to burn them. Once cashews start to brown, they burn quicky.
6. Add the cooked beans, liquid and all, to the vegetable mixture. Add the toasted cashews and the vinegar. Simmer for 30 minutes to blend the flavors.
7. Taste and adjust the seasonings.
8. You can serve the chili hot, just as it is, with fresh hot corn bread and butter. Or serve it Cabbagetown style: for each person put a small serving of cooked brown rice in the bottom of an ovenproof bowl. Ladle hot chili

over the rice, then sprinkle with grated
Cheddar cheese and extra toasted cashews.
Bake in the oven for 15 minutes or until the
cheese bubbles, then serve with corn bread.

Yield: Serves 6

June at staff dinner after the night shift

Tostadas

2 cups Craig's Refried Beans (page 23) or
    Mexican Potato Salad (page 61)
2 cups Uncooked Salsa (page 24)
Light vegetable oil
4 corn tortillas
2 cups grated Cheddar cheese
4 cups finely shredded lettuce or spinach
Sour cream or Guacamole (page 25)
Alfalfa sprouts
4 marinated artichoke hearts (optional)
Chopped black olives

A Cabbagetown tostada is a crisp-fried corn tortilla topped with refried beans or Mexican potato salad, melted Cheddar cheese, salad greens, sour cream or guacamole, black olives, and if we are feeling extravagant, marinated artichoke hearts. Tostadas are good for lunch.

1. First make the refried beans or potato salad and salsa.
2. To fry the tostada tortillas, pour the oil about 1/2-inch deep in a frying pan or wok. Heat the oil over medium heat until a tortilla dropped in it sizzles and floats. Fry 1 tortilla at a time. Use tongs to poke it down into the oil. Flip it once. It's done when you can hold it with the tongs, and trying to bend it against the edge of the pan, it feels stiff and brittle. Drain on a brown paper bag.
3. Arrange the tortillas on a baking tray. Cover each tortilla with a generous 1/2 cup of beans or potato salad. Sprinkle each with 1/2 cup Cheddar cheese. Bake in a preheated 350°F. oven for 15–20 minutes, until the cheese is melted and bubbly.
4. Put each baked tortilla on a serving plate. On top of it mound 1 cup shredded lettuce or spinach, 1/2 cup salsa, a generous dollop of sour cream or guacamole, and a mound of alfalfa sprouts. Nestle the artichoke hearts in the middle if you're using them, and sprinkle with chopped black olives. Serve immediately.

Yield: Serves 4

Varsha's Indian Dinners

Varsha walked into Cabbagetown one day with a sample Indian meal for us to taste. As we gobbled it up, she offered to cook delicious and genuinely Indian food in the restaurant.

Varsha also taught English to other wives of foreign grad students so they wouldn't feel so totally lost in America. During the last months she was here, Varsha wrote a cookbook called Salads of India *for the Crossing Press.*

Varsha would rock back and forth as she chopped vegetables in Cabbagetown. She was totally comfortable cooking massive quantities of food with a bunch of Americans in a big, unfamiliar kitchen. She was comfortable converting her classic Indian recipes to the natural foods ingredients we insisted on using. And everything she made was terrific.

When putting together an Indian meal, Varsha liked to include a bean dish (Indian Lentil Soup, Chick-pea Curry), a vegetable dish (Dry Potato Curry, Cauliflower Curry), a salad (Raita or Koshimbir), and rice, chappatis, or parathas. One dish should include yoghurt. If not, she served plain yoghurt on the side. For fancier meals she included a fried food (Onion Pakoras), papadams (wafers you buy in an Indian store, then fry up), and chutney.

Here are two Cabbagetown Indian dinners she suggests you can cook for starters. The first dinner is Cabbage Dal (a lentil and cabbage soup, page 83), Dry Potato Curry (page 171), Cucumber Raita (page 173). and Parathas (page 176). The second dinner is Chick-pea Curry (page 167), Onion Pakoras (page 27), Koshimbir (page 174), Lemon Rice (page 172), and plain yoghurt. It's best to serve a meal all at once rather than in courses. Varsha feels that any American dessert, especially ice cream, goes well with Indian meals.

Buy all the spices needed for these recipes. They'll give your food a genuine Indian taste, and you'll use them over and over. Several years ago I had trouble finding asafetida, but today it is readily available in Asian food stores. All the other spices are quite easy to find.

This chapter is dedicated to Varsha, a generous human being and a great cook.

Chick Pea Curry

2 cups uncooked chick-peas, sorted for stones and rinsed
10 cups water
3–4 whole cloves
2–3 cardamon pods
1-inch piece stick cinnamon
10–12 black peppercorns
3 tablespoons light vegetable oil
2 whole cloves
1 cardamon pod
1-inch piece stick cinnamon
2 onions, finely chopped
4 cloves of garlic, finely chopped
1/2-inch piece fresh ginger, finely chopped
3 tomatoes, chopped
1 teaspoon salt
1 1/2 teaspoons ground cumin
1/2 teaspoon ground coriander
Chopped fresh coriander leaves (optional)

This dish was one of the first things Varsha learned to cook. Chick-peas are tasty and popular with everyone; cooking them is basically foolproof.

1. Measure the chick-peas, water, 3–4 whole cloves, 2–3 cardamon pods, 1-inch piece stick cinnamon and 10–12 peppercorns into a large pot. Bring to a boil, then reduce the heat and simmer, partially covered, for 2–3 hours, until the chick-peas are very tender. Pour through a colander to drain, and save the chick-pea cooking liquid.

2. In a medium-size frying pan, heat the oil. Add the remaining cloves, cardamon pod, and cinnamon. Cook until the spices swell up, then add the onions. Sauté until the onions are brown, then add the garlic and ginger. Sauté for 2–3 minutes more. Add the tomatoes, and cook for about 10 minutes, until the tomatoes are soft.

3. Add the drained chick-peas, salt, cumin, and coriander. Cook for 10–15 minutes, adding chick-pea cooking liquid as needed to make a saucy consistency.

4. Serve garnished with chopped fresh coriander leaves, if available.

KIDNEY BEAN CURRY
Substitute 2 cups uncooked kidney beans for the chick-peas. Increase the ginger to a 1-inch piece, finely chopped.

Yield: Serves 6

Greg's Chick Peas

2 cups uncooked chick-peas, sorted for
  stones and rinsed
10 cups water
2 tablespoons light vegetable oil
1 onion, cut in crescents
1 teaspoon cayenne
1/4 cup butter
1 teaspoon salt

This recipe is a little hotter than Varsha's and
very buttery. Try both. They're equally
delicious.

1. Measure the chick-peas and water into a
large pot. Bring to a boil, then reduce the heat
and simmer, partially covered, for 2–3 hours,
until the chick-peas are very tender. Pour
through a colander to drain, and save the
chick-pea cooking liquid.
2. In a medium-size frying pan, heat the oil.
Add the onion and cook over high heat,
stirring frequently, until some of the slices are
quite brown.
3. Add the cayenne, then immediately add the
butter, and stir until it is all melted. Add the
drained chick-peas, salt, and a little chick-pea
cooking liquid.
4. Simmer, stirring occasionally, for 30–60
minutes. Add more chick-pea cooking liquid a
little at a time, and continue to cook until the
chick-peas are slightly mushy, the flavors are
blended, and the whole mixture has a stew-
like consistency with a little gravy around the
chick-peas.

Yield: Serves 6

Greg doing the books

Cauliflower Curry

1/4 cup light vegetable oil
2 teaspoons black mustard seeds
1/4 teaspoon asafetida
1 teaspoon turmeric
1/2 cup dried unsweetened or grated fresh
  coconut
1 fresh hot pepper, finely chopped
4 cloves of garlic, finely chopped
1/2-inch piece fresh ginger, finely chopped
2 onions, chopped
1 quart canned tomatoes or 6–8 fresh ripe
  tomatoes, chopped
2 teaspoons salt
1 teaspoon molasses
1 tablespoon ground cumin
1 tablespoon ground coriander
1 head cauliflower, cut in bite-size pieces
1 cup water
2 green peppers, chopped, seeds and all

According to Varsha, "It's hard to know that the vegetable is cauliflower. Once someone called this chicken curry." This dish is good eaten with plain boiled rice or with parathas.

1. In a soup pot, heat the oil until a mustard seed dropped in it sizzles. Pour in the mustard seeds and cook until they pop. Lower the heat and stir frequently so you don't burn any of the seeds. Stir in the asafetida, then the turmeric, then the coconut. Add the chopped hot pepper, then the garlic and ginger and cook for about 5 minutes. Stir frequently so nothing sticks. If anything does start to stick, add more oil.
2. Add the onions. Stir and cook for 10 minutes. Crush the canned tomatoes by hand to get small pieces, or chop the fresh tomatoes. Add to the pot along with the salt, molasses, cumin, and coriander.
3. Add the cauliflower and water. Cover and cook for 20 minutes, stirring occasionally.
4. Add the peppers. Cover and cook for 30 minutes, stirring occasionally.
5. Taste and adjust the seasonings.

CAULIFLOWER GREEN PEA CURRY
Add 2 cups fresh or frozen green peas about 15 minutes before you finish cooking.

POTATO GREEN PEA CURRY
Substitute 4 potatoes, cut in cubes, for the cauliflower. Add 2 cups green peas 15 minutes before you finish cooking.

Yield: Serves 6

Dry Potato Curry

6 potatoes
1/4 cup light vegetable oil
2 teaspoons black mustard seeds
1/2 teaspoon asafetida
1 teaspoon turmeric
3 onions, chopped
2 teaspoons ground cumin
2 teaspoons ground coriander
1/2 teaspoon cayenne
Juice of 1/2 lemon
1 teaspoon salt

This is very easy to prepare and makes a good all-purpose dish. Potatoes and Indian spices are meant for each other.

1. Scrub the potatoes well but do not peel. Cook in water to cover until done but still firm, about 30 minutes after the water boils. Cut into bite-size pieces.
2. In a fairly large frying pan, heat the oil over medium heat. Add the mustard seeds and stir until they pop but do not burn. Add the asafetida and turmeric, then immediately add the onions. Stir until the onions are cooked.
3. Add the cumin, coriander, cayenne, and lemon juice. Then mix in the potatoes and salt, and cook for a few minutes.
4. Taste and serve immediately.

Yield: Serves 6

Lemon Rice

2 cups uncooked brown rice
3 1/2 cups water
2 teaspoons salt
1/2 teaspoon turmeric
3–4 whole cloves
10–12 black peppercorns
1 bay leaf
2 tablespoons light vegetable oil
1 1/2 teaspoons black mustard seeds
1/2 teaspoon asafetida
2 fresh hot peppers, finely chopped
3 onions, chopped
1 cup roasted peanuts
2 green peppers, chopped
2 cups fresh or frozen green peas
2 tablespoons ground cumin
1 1/2 tablespoons ground coriander
1/2 teaspoon cayenne
Juice of 1 lemon
1 1/2 teaspoons salt
1 teaspoon molasses
1/2 cup finely chopped scallions
Chopped fresh coriander leaves (optional)

This yellow rice is hearty and unusual enough to be served by itself, as a main dish along with an Indian soup or salad, or better still, serve it as part of an Indian feast. Any leftovers are delicious the next day.

1. In a medium-size pot, mix the rice, water, salt, turmeric, cloves, peppercorns, and bay leaf. Cover and cook on low heat until all the water is absorbed, about 40 minutes.
2. In a large soup pot, heat the oil. Fry the mustard seeds until they pop. Add the asafetida and fry, stirring quickly.
3. In this order add the hot peppers, onions, peanuts, peppers, and peas. Cook for 10 minutes.
4. Mix in the cumin, coriander, and cayenne.
5. Add the lemon juice, salt, molasses, and scallions.
6. Mix in the rice and stir well.
7. Serve garnished with chopped fresh coriander leaves, if available.

Yield: Serves 6

Cucumber Raita

1 teaspoon cumin seeds
2 cucumbers or tomatoes, chopped
1 red or white onion, cut in crescents
2 cups plain yoghurt
2 teaspoons finely chopped fresh mint
1/4 teaspoon salt
1/4 teaspoon paprika

This is a cooling yoghurt salad to serve with an Indian meal.

1. Toast the cumin seeds lightly in a dry frying pan and mash them slightly with the back of a wooden spoon.
2. Mix together all the ingredients.
3. Taste and adjust the seasonings.
4. Refrigerate for 1–2 hours before serving. This raita does not keep well, so plan to eat it fresh.

RICHER CUCUMBER RAITA
Omit the onion and add 2 tablespoons sour cream.

CARROT RAITA
Substitute 2 carrots, boiled and mashed, in place of the cucumbers or tomatoes. Substitute 2 teaspoons finely chopped fresh coriander leaves for the mint.

BEET RAITA
Substitute 2 beets, boiled and mashed, in place of the cucumbers or tomatoes. Substitute 2 teaspoons finely chopped fresh coriander leaves for the mint.

Yield: Serves 6

Koshimbir

1 cup grated fresh coconut
1 cup peanuts, raw or roasted
2 cucumbers, peeled and finely chopped
2 tomatoes, finely chopped
Juice of 1 lemon
2 tablespoons light vegetable oil
1 teaspoon black mustard seeds
Pinch asafetida
Pinch turmeric
1 fresh hot pepper, finely chopped
1 teaspoon salt

This distinctive salad, with fresh coconut and peanut meal, is served in small bowls along with an Indian meal. Make it right before serving. You can chop the vegetables and prepare the coconut and peanut meal in advance, but don't toss the salad until the last instant. Also eat it all up at one sitting. The freshness and fun of it is totally lost on the second day.

1. Here's Varsha in *Salads of India* on coconut. "Don't try to substitute dried coconut flakes for fresh coconut. The addition of fresh coconut is what makes our salads distinctive. Be careful to choose coconuts without cracks. Store in the refrigerator. To crack them open, hit them on any hard surface like the front steps or the sidewalk. (I use a hammer.) Use a knife to separate the meat from the hard shell. This takes a little force. Grate the meat. Store any grated coconut you don't use immediately in the freezer in sealed plastic bags."

2. Make the peanuts into roasted peanut meal. If you're starting with raw peanuts, roast them in a dry frying pan for about 10 minutes, or until dark spots appear. Stir frequently so the peanuts don't burn. Allow to cool. Grind them in a grain mill, or at low speed in a blender or food processor. Don't grind too fast or you will make peanut butter. If you're starting with roasted peanuts, grind them as above.

3. With your hands, squeeze all the juice you can get out of the chopped cucumbers. "Cucumber juice is good for the complexion," says Varsha.

4. Mix together the coconut, peanut meal, cucumbers, tomatoes, and lemon juice.
5. In a small pot, heat the oil until a mustard seed dropped in it pops. Add the mustard seeds, asafetida, turmeric, and chopped hot pepper, and fry for about 30 seconds. Pour over the vegetable mixture. Mix in the salt.
6. Taste and adjust the seasonings. Chill in the refrigerator until serving.

CABBAGE KOSHIMBIR
Substitute a medium-size wedge of cabbage, very finely chopped, for 1 cucumber and 1 tomato.

Yield: Serves 6

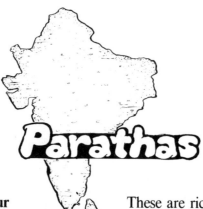

Parathas

1 cup whole wheat bread flour
1 cup whole wheat pastry flour
1 teaspoon salt
About 3/4 cup cold water
Whole wheat pastry flour for dusting the
  counter
1/2 cup finely chopped scallions
Light vegetable oil

These are rich Indian flat breads, made with oil in the dough. Varsha says that in India when girls start learning to roll out parathas, they always try for a round shape. Since you can get them round only with years of practice, you can easily tell the inexperienced cooks—their parathas are shaped like India.

1. Mix the flours with the salt in a medium-size mixing bowl. Add cold water until you get a kneadable dough. Knead the dough on a lightly floured counter until the dough sticks together. Divide it into lemon-size balls.

2. Roll out the balls 1 at a time as follows, dusting the counter with flour only as needed. First roll out the dough until it is the size of a small saucer. Put a teaspoon of oil on it, and smooth the oil over the surface. Sprinkle with 1 tablespoon chopped scallions. Fold the paratha in half and press the edges. Fold in half again. (Now it is wedge-shaped.) Roll out the wedge to 4 times its size, aiming for a final round shape.

3. Heat a cast iron frying pan. Put in 1 paratha and roast it for a couple of minutes on both sides. Add 1 teaspoon oil to the pan and roast each side again until brown spots appear. Taste your first paratha to make sure it's done. Sometimes the paratha puffs up. (Varsha says that when she makes them they always puff up, but for novices they may not.) Continue to roast all the parathas. Serve immediately.

Yield: 6–8 parathas. Serves 6

Sunday Brunch

Except for one year, I've always worked the Sunday brunch shift. It's my weekly act of devotion to Cabbagetown. The hardest part about it is getting up, but once I'm outside and walking to the restaurant everything is fine. There's a certain Sunday freshness in the air, and all of Ithaca is quiet.

Preparing for Sunday brunch is full of rituals—all done at high speed. We chop mushrooms, make home fries, make huge batches of muffins, pile up stacks of coffee filters, pile up stacks of eggs. Then we turn the sign to "Open," and if conditions are right—fairly decent weather, Cornell in session, no big concert Saturday night to make people sleep late—Sunday brunch is the busiest meal of the week. Many of my employees who normally wouldn't touch coffee drink it while working brunch just to keep pace with the scene.

I pay special homage to those fearless Cabbages who through the years have done "Sunday brunch back counter." The back counter person makes all the omelettes, huevos rancheros, scrambled tofu, and special egg orders. This person must not only be skillful at cooking eggs, but must have nerves of steel. My position at Sunday brunch is "Front counter." I shout out orders, serve muffins and fruit, and rush out into the dining room to help. This is challenging, but it is nothing like back counter.

When brunch is over, we scrub all the sticky pans, scrub up the eggs that have flown all over the stove, sweep the eggshells and cantaloupe off the floor, and collapse.

The food at brunch is some of our best: our Sunday brunch muffins, our Huevos Rancheros, inspirational omelettes by Matthew who was probably the best omelette cook I've ever met. So make a pot of your favorite coffee, always serve it with heavy cream, make some muffins, and sit down with a copy of the New York Times. *Or come visit us at Cabbagetown.*

Cabbagetown Omelettes

The ability to make a great omelette comes only with practice. I remember one dramatic moment when Matthew was teaching my brother Kurt to make omelettes. Kurt was nervous. Matthew stood by the stove with his white apron, arms crossed over his chest. Kurt managed to make several good omelettes, then flipped one so it landed half in the pan and the rest splattered on the stove. Matthew reached over, grabbed the pan, and whacked it upside down on the garbage can to clean it out. He put the pan back on the stove in about half a second. "Make another one."

Matthew is a fiery hot-tempered cook. Although he's moved back to his home in Buffalo, New York, he taught enough people at Cabbagetown to make omelettes that his methods and his standards still abide. I'll describe his technique for you.

OMELETTE PAN
First you need an omelette pan. Since each omelette maker at Cabbagetown prefers a different pan, I've stopped recommending any special type. I'd suggest going to a kitchen supply store with a wide selection of omelette pans, then buying the one that appeals to you, for whatever reason. Season your pan and keep it seasoned by using it only for omelettes. Each time you use it, clean it by sprinkling it with salt, rubbing it around with a paper towel to loosen all stuck particles, then wiping it clean with another paper towel. Rub it lightly with oil before storing it away.

PREPARING TO MAKE OMELETTES
When you're going to make omelettes, first make your omelette filling. Some of our favorite recipes follow. Grate the cheeses and make any sauces you're going to use. You want to have everything ready.

At Cabbagetown we make a 3-egg omelette for each person. It's a substantial size, and it flips nicely in a standard omelette pan. At home you might want to make a 3-egg omelette for each hungry person, and cut the omelettes in half to feed not-so-hungry people.

OMELETTE METHOD

When you're ready to begin making omelettes, surround yourself with the following:

Omelette pan on the stove
A medium-size mixing bowl
A whisk
1 tablespoon butter for each omelette
3 eggs for each omelette
A fork
1/2 cup filling for each omelette
1/2 cup grated cheese for each omelette
Sauce as desired
Serving plates

Make omelettes 1 at a time as follows.

1. Turn on the heat under your omelette pan so the flame of a gas burner is about 3/8 inch high, or turn an electric burner to medium. Drop in 1 tablespoon butter.

2. As you wait for the butter to melt completely, crack 3 eggs into a mixing bowl and whisk them vigorously. As soon as the melted butter starts to foam, pour the eggs into the pan.

3. As the eggs cook, lift the edges of the omelette with the fork, and tilt the pan so uncooked egg runs down under the cooked part. It it is cooking too fast and making you nervous, turn down the heat a little. If it is taking forever, turn the heat up a little. As soon as the eggs are cooked enough that the omelette looks slightly firm, shake it around a little in the pan to be sure it is not stuck anywhere. If it is, pry it loose gently with the fork. Then flip the omelette completely over so that it lands squarely back in the pan with a delightful slap. This is easier said than done, and where practice is necessary.

4. Remove the pan from the heat right after you flip the omelette. Put the cheese in a stripe down the center of the omelette, and cover the cheese with the filling. Roll the omelette by sliding it to the edge of the pan, then rolling it out onto a serving plate. If it doesn't roll up nicely, use your hand to shape it gently.

5. If you're making several omelettes and want to serve them all at once, put each omelette on its plate into a warm oven.

6. Melt another tablespoon of butter in your omelette pan, and continue making omelettes in the same way.

7. When you're ready to serve, ladle a sauce in a saddle across the center of each omelette. Garnish and serve immediately.

Yield: 3-egg omelettes. Serves 1–2

FILLING

6 ounces mushrooms, sliced (2 cups)
2 tablespoons butter
Freshly ground black pepper
Fresh lemon juice
1 tablespoon butter

OMELETTES

2 tablespoons butter
6 eggs
1 cup grated Swiss cheese

We fry mushrooms in small batches at high heat so the mushrooms are seared and keep most of their juice.

1. Rinse the mushrooms until clean. Slice just a bit off the bottom of each stem to remove any dirt. Then slice each mushroom in fairly thick slices, about 3–4 slices to a mushroom.
2. In a medium-size frying pan, melt 2 tablespoons of butter until it is bubbling. Toss in 1 cup of mushrooms and sauté over high heat, stirring with a wooden spoon to keep the mushrooms from sticking. Grind in a little black pepper and sprinkle with fresh lemon juice. When the mushrooms are golden brown and succulent, after 3–4 minutes of cooking, remove to a bowl.
3. In the same frying pan, melt 1 more tablespoon butter, and sauté the second cup of mushrooms in the same way. Add the first batch of mushrooms and sauté them together for about 1 minute. Turn off the heat.
4. When you're ready to make omelettes, heat the mushrooms until they are warm.
5. Make each omelette according to the directions on pages 179–180, using 1 tablespoon butter and 3 eggs for each. Sprinkle 1/2 cup grated Swiss cheese down the center of each. Top with mushrooms, and roll up. Make a little cut in the top of each omelette and stand up 2 nice looking mushroom slices as a garnish. Serve immediately.

Yield: 2 omelettes. Serves 2–4

Spinach Ricotta Omelettes

FILLING

1 tablespoon butter

1 onion, diced

1 tablespoon olive oil

5–6 ounces fresh spinach, chopped (4 cups)

1/4 cup coarsely chopped black olives

1 teaspoon dried basil or 2 teaspoons finely chopped fresh basil

1/2 teaspoon freshly ground black pepper

1/2 cup whole milk ricotta cheese

OMELETTES

2 tablespoons butter

6 eggs

1 cup grated Swiss cheese

Fresh whole milk ricotta is a must for these omelettes.

1. In a medium-size frying pan, melt 1 tablespoon butter. Add the onion and sauté until sweet and translucent, about 3–4 minutes.

2. Add the olive oil, then add the chopped spinach 2 cups at a time, cooking down after each addition. Add the olives, basil, and pepper, and saute for 1 minute.

3. Add the ricotta and heat until warm, about 2 minutes. Taste and adjust the seasonings. You might want to add more pepper or a pinch of salt. Remove from the heat until you're ready to make omelettes. If the filling has cooled down, warm it again before filling omelettes.

4. Make each omelette using 1 tablespoon butter and 3 eggs according to the directions on pages 179–180. Sprinkle 1/2 cup grated Swiss cheese in a stripe down the center of each, top with a generous 1/2 cup of the spinach filling, and roll up. Serve immediately, with home fries and whole wheat toast.

Yield: 2 omelettes. Serves 2–4

Apple Cheddar Omelettes

FILLING

2 tablespoons butter
3 apples, sliced
Juice of 1/2 lemon
1/4 teaspoon cinnamon
Pinch nutmeg
1 teaspoon honey, maple syrup, or Grand
   Marnier (optional)

OMELETTES

2 tablespoons butter
6 eggs
1 cup grated Cheddar cheese
1/2 cup sour cream (optional)

Omelettes filled with lightly sautéed apples hit the spot in the fall during apple season.

1. In a medium-size frying pan, melt 2 tablespoons butter. Add the apples and sauté until just tender, about 4 minutes. Add the lemon juice and cook for 1 minute more, until the juice is absorbed. Stir in the spices. Turn off the heat.
2. Taste. If the filling is a little too tart, add 1 teaspoon honey, maple syrup, or Grand Marnier to sweeten it.
3. When you're ready to make omelettes, turn on the heat just long enough to warm the apples.
4. Make each omelette using 1 tablespoon butter and 3 eggs according to the directions on pages 179–180. Sprinkle 1/2 cup grated Cheddar cheese in a stripe down the center of each. Top with a generous 1/2 cup of the apple filling, and roll up. Top with sour cream if you're using it, and garnish with a sautéed apple slice. Serve immediately.

PEACHES AND SOUR CREAM
OMELETTE
Substitute peaches for the apples. Omit the Cheddar cheese. Top with sour cream.

Yield: 2 omelettes. Serves 2–4

Ratatouille Omelettes

FILLING

3 tablespoons olive oil
1 eggplant, cut in bite-size cubes (6 cups)
1 zucchini, cut in bite-size cubes (3–4 cups)
Freshly ground black pepper
4 cloves of garlic
1 bay leaf
2 tablespoons olive oil
2 onions, chopped
2 green peppers, cut in fairly large pieces
1 quart canned tomatoes or 6 fresh ripe
  tomatoes, chopped
1 teaspoon dried basil or 1 tablespoon
  finely chopped fresh basil
1/2 teaspoon dried or finely chopped fresh
  thyme

FOR EACH OMELETTE

1 tablespoon butter
3 eggs
1/2 cup grated Swiss cheese
1/4 cup sour cream or 2 tablespoons Garlic
  Herb Mayonnaise (page 185) (optional)
Black olives (optional)

Ratatouille is a richly flavored vegetable mixture containing eggplant, zucchini, and tomatoes. There's no point in making a small amount of ratatouille, so plan to freeze some for future omelettes, or serve it as a side dish for lunch or dinner.

1. In a large frying pan, heat 3 tablespoons olive oil. Add the eggplant and zucchini, and sauté for about 5 minutes, until tender. Grind in a little black pepper. Remove to a bowl.
2. Chop together the garlic and bay leaf to make a paste.
3. In the same frying pan, heat another 2 tablespoons olive oil. Add the onions and peppers and sauté for 2–3 minutes, until they just begin to become tender. Add the garlic-bay leaf paste, then the tomatoes, then the basil and thyme. Simmer for 10 minutes.
4. Return the eggplant and zucchini to the vegetable mixture in the frying pan. Simmer for about 20 minutes to blend the flavors.
5. Keep simmering over low heat.
6. Make each omelette using 1 tablespoon butter and 3 eggs according to the directions on page 179–180. Sprinkle 1/2 cup grated Swiss cheese down the center of each, top with a generous 1/2 cup of the ratatouille filling, and roll up. Top with sauce and a black olive garnish if desired, and serve immediately with homemade whole wheat bread and butter.

Yield: 8 cups. Filling for 12 omelettes, or serves 6 as a vegetable dish

Garlic Herb Mayonnaise

1 egg
1/2 teaspoon salt
Juice of 1/2 lemon
1 cup light vegetable oil
2 cloves of garlic, finely chopped
1 cup finely chopped fresh green herbs
1 teaspoon freshly ground black pepper

This is a delicious sauce for any vegetable omelette.

1. Whisk or blend the egg with the salt and 1 tablespoon of the lemon juice until creamy.
2. Whisking or blending constantly, add about 1/2–2/3 of the oil in a slow trickle. At some point the mayonnaise will "take," or become much thicker.
3. After the mayonnaise thickens, continue beating in the remaining oil alternately with the rest of the lemon juice. Blend or whisk in the garlic.
4. Stir in the chopped green herbs and the black pepper. You do not want to blend these, since the texture is nicer for omelettes if the herbs are just chopped. Taste and adjust the seasonings.
5. Pour it in a saddle over the center of an omelette.

Yield: 1 1/2 cups

Broccoli Hollandaise Omelettes

FILLING

1 stalk broccoli, cut in bite-size pieces (2 cups)

2 tablespoons butter

1 onion, cut in crescents

1/4 teaspoon dried or finely chopped fresh tarragon

1/4 teaspoon dried or finely chopped fresh thyme

1/2 teaspoon dried dill weed or 1 tablespoon finely chopped fresh dill

Freshly ground black pepper

OMELETTES

2 tablespoons butter

6 eggs

1 cup grated Swiss cheese

1/2 cup Hollandaise Sauce (page 187)

There's no doubt about it—the best omelettes have hollandaise sauce poured over them. At Cabbagetown we especially like serving hollandaise over omelettes with steamed vegetable fillings.

1. First prepare the hollandaise sauce.
2. Steam or blanch the broccoli for about 5 minutes, until tender. Drain and set aside.
3. In a medium-size frying pan, melt 2 tablespoons butter. Add the onion and sauté until translucent, 3–4 minutes. Add the broccoli, herbs, and pepper. Cook over low heat for about 1 minute, stirring constantly, to blend the flavors. If the mixture starts to stick, stir in a little of the broccoli cooking water. Remove from the heat until you're ready to make omelettes. If the mixture has cooled down, warm it again before filling omelettes.
4. Make each omelette using 1 tablespoon butter and 3 eggs according to the directions on page 179–180. Sprinkle 1/2 cup grated Swiss cheese in a stripe down the center of each, top with a generous 1/2 cup of the broccoli filling, and roll up. Ladle about 1/4 cup of hollandaise Sauce in a saddle across the center of each omelette.

VEGETABLE HOLLANDAISE
OMELETTES
Substitute steamed asparagus, cauliflower, green beans, or brussels sprouts for the broccoli.

Yield: 2 omelettes. Serves 2–4

Hollandaise Sauce

1/2 pound butter (Unsalted butter is traditional and subtly better-tasting, but salted butter is fine.)
2 tablespoons red wine vinegar
4 egg yolks
Fresh lemon juice
Salt
Cayenne

The following is Anne's version, via French cooking school. Says Anne, "Boy, what a lot of work! But it tastes great."

1. Melt the butter over moderate heat in a medium-size pot. Ladle away the foam, boil, ladle away foam, etc. until most of the foam is removed. Be careful not to burn the butter. Set aside and let cool.
2. Boil the vinegar until it evaporates down to 1 teaspoon. This happens in no time.
3. Whisk the egg yolks in a bowl over boiling water. Take the bowl away from the heat often to ensure that the eggs are not solidifying on the sides of the bowl. Add the vinegar after you've whisked for about 1 minute. Whisk until the mixture becomes a lighter yellow and drops off the whisk in a ribbon that doesn't dissolve instantly.
4. Slowly, drop by drop at first, ladle the butter into the egg yolks, whisking vigorously all the time. After you have added a significant amount, you can add it faster. Do not add the milky residue at the bottom of the pan. "Pitch it," says Anne. "Use it creatively in cooking," says me. Whisk! Whisk! The sauce will be thick, but not quite as thick as mayonnaise.
5. Add lemon juice, salt, and cayenne to taste. Serve immediately.

Yield: 1 cup. Serves 4–6

Huevos Rancheros

2 cups salsa (I recommend Cooked Salsa,
  (page 149)
2 tablespoons butter
4 corn tortillas
2 tablespoons butter
4 eggs
Salt
Black pepper
2 cups finely grated Cheddar cheese
Sour cream and black olives (optional)

At various times the Sunday brunch crews use silly gimmicks to keep their energy up through the meal. One crew used to cry out "Huevos!" (pronounced "wavos") in unison every time they got an order. Huevos are a wonderful way to start a Sunday—traditional fare with a slight jolt.

1. First make the salsa and keep it hot on the stove.
2. Next fry the tortillas. Melt 2 tablespoons butter in a medium-size frying pan. Fry each corn tortilla in the butter by cooking the tortilla on 1 side until it just starts to get limp, then turning it over and frying it 1–2 seconds on the other side until it's all soft. Arrange 2 cooked tortillas, slightly overlapping, on each serving plate.
3. Melt 1 tablespoon butter in the same frying pan. Cook 2 eggs in the butter—fried, scrambled, etc. Sprinkle lightly with salt and pepper, and slide onto the tortillas. Melt 1 more tablespoon butter in the pan and cook the remaining 2 eggs. Slide onto the other plate of tortillas.
4. Sprinkle the eggs with grated Cheddar cheese, top with hot salsa, and serve immediately. If you're feeling extravagant, top each serving with a big dollop of sour cream and some chopped black olives. Cabbagetown customers usually order coffee or Mexican beer with huevos.

HUEVOS NO EGGS

This is the most amusing order we get at brunch. Many of our customers don't eat eggs, but like everything else about huevos rancheros. When they order "Huevos, no eggs," which translates as "Eggs, no eggs," we either leave out the eggs and top the fried tortillas with cheese and salsa, or we substitute 1 cup of hot home fries (page 194) for the eggs.

Yield: Serves 2

Scrambled Tofu

4 cups Marinated Tofu (double the recipe on page 54)

4 potatoes

1 stalk broccoli, cut in bite-size pieces (2–3 cups)

1 tablespoon light vegetable oil

3 carrots, sliced

1 teaspoon dried marjoram or 1 tablespoon finely chopped fresh marjoram

1 tablespoon light vegetable oil

2 onions, cut in crescents

2 cloves of garlic, finely chopped

1 teaspoon dried or finely chopped fresh thyme

1/2 teaspoon dried or finely chopped fresh tarragon

2 cups fresh or frozen green peas or corn

1 tablespoon light vegetable oil

1 tablespoon dark sesame oil

1 tablespoon tamari or soy sauce

Tamari-Roasted Almonds (page 59)

I invented this tofu dish for brunch customers who don't eat eggs, but it's caught on with everyone. You cook tofu and vegetables separately, mix them all together, then fry them up with extra dark sesame oil and tamari. This dish is also good for dinner.

1. First prepare the tofu. Put in a large bowl.
2. Scrub the potatoes well but do not peel. Cook in water to cover until tender, about 30 minutes after the water boils. Dice into bite-size cubes. Add to the tofu in the bowl.
3. Steam or blanch the broccoli for about 5 minutes, until just tender. Add to the bowl.
4. In a medium-size frying pan, heat 1 tablespoon oil. Add the carrots and sauté for about 3 minutes, then add 1/4 cup of water to steam until the carrots are tender and the water is absorbed. This takes about 5 minutes more. Stir in the marjoram. Add to the vegetables in the bowl.
5. In the same frying pan, heat 1 tablespoon oil. Add the onions and garlic and sauté until limp, 3–4 minutes. Add the thyme, tarragon, and peas or corn. Sauté for 2–3 minutes to thaw the frozen vegetables or to cook the fresh ones very lightly. Remove to the bowl.
6. At this stage you can cover the mixture and refrigerate until ready to serve, or you can fry it up right away. Heat 1 tablespoon oil in a frying pan. Add the tofu-vegetable mixture from the bowl. Cook until hot, stirring frequently. When hot, stir in 1 tablespoon dark sesame oil and 1 tablespoon tamari or soy sauce. Taste and adjust the seasonings.
7. Serve immediately, sprinkled with almonds.

VEGETABLE SCRAMBLED TOFU

You can add many other vegetables. I like steamed cauliflower, steamed green beans, lightly sautéed zucchini, and sautéed mushrooms.

Yield: Serves 4

Grandma Rachel's Potato Latkes (Pancakes)

5 potatoes
1 onion
1 egg, beaten
1 teaspoon salt
1/4 teaspoon black pepper
1/4 cup whole wheat pastry flour
1 teaspoon baking powder
Light vegetable oil for frying
Sour cream
Prepared horseradish
Applesauce

Jill says, "I learned this recipe sitting in my Grandma's kitchen. I have seen her make them so many times that the first time I made them on my own, I felt totally at home. I make them virtually the same way that she does, except I wash the potatoes thoroughly instead of peeling them." The first time we served these at Cabbagetown, Jill went around the dining room smiling, "Ess. Ess."

1. Scrub the potatoes well but do not peel.
2. Grate the potatoes. The texture of the grated potatoes is the secret to good potato latkes. You should grate them by hand on a stand up grater. The surface to use looks like pencil points pushed through the metal. It's a lot of work, but it's worth it. Be careful not to grate your knuckles. Put the grated potatoes in a medium-size mixing bowl. After the potatoes are grated, they will be a thick watery mush. If they are too watery, pour out the excess water until the final texture is thicker than pancake batter, but not dry. The grated potatoes will brown somewhat as they sit. This is natural when they are exposed to air. For this reason the potatoes are usually grated close to frying time. If you must grate them in advance, sprinkle a little of the whole wheat pastry flour over the top to retard browning.
3. Grate in the onion.
4. Next add the beaten egg, salt, and pepper. Add the rest of the flour and the baking powder. Now the mixture should be firm enough to make nice heaping spoonfuls, but not stiff or dry. It should look similar to

applesauce.

5. Fry the latkes in your best-seasoned frying pan. The better the pan is seasoned, the better the latkes, since they won't stick. Heat oil about 1/4 inch deep in the pan. When the oil is hot, drop in heaping tablespoonfuls of batter. Fry each latke until it is brown around the edges, about 3 minutes. Turn it over. Continue frying on the other side for 2–3 minutes more, until the latkes are a rich deep brown on both sides. Place on paper towels or a brown paper bag to drain off excess oil.

6. Potato latkes are best eaten immediately after frying, but in a pinch they can be reheated on a baking tray in the oven. Serve latkes hot with sour cream and prepared horseradish, or with applesauce, or with all 3.

Yield: 20 latkes. Serves 4

Cabbagetown Home Fries

6 potatoes
2 onions
2 cloves of garlic
3–4 tablespoons butter
1/4 teaspoon paprika
Pinch cayenne
1/2 teaspoon salt
Freshly ground black pepper

Anne, our extraordinary French pastry and hollandaise sauce cook, was also known for her home fries. When asked for her secret, she'd always reply, "Butter and salt."

1. Scrub the potatoes well but do not peel. Cook in water to cover until just tender, about 30 minutes after the water boils. Dice into large cubes.
2. Chop the onions into large pieces. You want the pieces large enough to hold their shape and to be recognizable after frying. Chop the garlic finely.
3. In a medium-size frying pan, melt 3 tablespoons butter. Add the onions and garlic and sauté until the onions are soft, 3–4 minutes. Add the potatoes, spices, salt, and pepper. Sauté, stirring frequently, until the potatoes are lightly browned and starting to get crusty, about 10 minutes. Add an additional 1 tablespoon butter if the potatoes start to stick.
4. Taste and adjust the seasonings. Serve hot, garnished with a sprig of parsley.

Yield: Serves 4

Cinnamon Buns

DOUGH

2 cups milk
1/2 cup butter
3/4 cup honey
Grated rind of 1 lemon
1 tablespoon active dry yeast
2 eggs, lightly beaten
3–4 cups whole wheat bread flour

FILLING

1/2 cup butter, at room temperature
1 cup honey
Grated rind of 2 oranges
2 teaspoons cinnamon
1 cup walnuts, coarsely chopped
1 cup raisins

We make cinnamon buns for Sunday brunch when we're feeling ambitious.

1. In a small pot, heat the milk and butter until the butter is melted.
2. Measure the honey and lemon rind into a bread bowl. Pour in the hot milk-butter mixture and stir until the honey is dissolved. While it's still warm, drop in the yeast. Leave the milk-yeast mixture for about 5 minutes, while the yeast dissolves and begins to foam.
3. Stir in the eggs, then about 3 cups of flour, enough to make a loose dough.
4. Allow to rise in a warm spot for 1 hour.
5. Turn the dough onto a floured counter, and knead in additional flour only until the dough holds together in a ball. You want the dough to be a little gooey and difficult to work with so your pastries will be lighter. Flour the counter well, and using a rolling pin, roll out the dough into the largest rectangle you can make, about 12 inches by 24 inches.
6. Cream together the butter, honey, orange rind, and cinnamon for the filling. Spread evenly over the dough. Sprinkle on the walnuts and the raisins.
7. Roll up the dough into a long cylinder. Cut it into slices each about 1 inch thick—18–24 slices. Place slices in a well-buttered 9-inch by 13-inch baking dish, or 2 or 3 pie plates.
8. Allow to rise in a warm spot for 1 hour until more than double. Bake in a preheated 350°F. oven for 30–40 minutes, until the buns are evenly browned.

Yield: 18–24 buns

Sunday Brunch Muffins

2 cups whole wheat pastry flour
1 tablespoon baking powder
1/4 teaspoon salt
2 teaspoons cinnamon
1/4 teaspoon nutmeg or ground cardamon
1/2 teaspoon allspice or powdered ginger
1/2 cup raisins or chopped dates
1/2 cup walnuts or almonds, coarsely
  chopped
Grated rind of 2 oranges
1 cup chopped fresh fruit (apples, pears,
  peaches, bananas, blueberries, or
  cranberries)
2 eggs
1/2 cup honey
1 cup milk
1 teaspoon vanilla or almond extract
1/4 cup butter, melted

For a long time I thought I couldn't make Cabbagetown muffins at home. But I've finally worked out the recipe, and here it is. One trick is to make the muffins as big as you possibly can. Big muffins are delightful because they have a neat crusty outside and a warm tender inside. If you want to stagger out of bed on Sunday morning and bake muffins without having to think, you can make a muffin mix the night before. Mix together the dry ingredients in one bowl or covered refrigerator container and the wet ingredients in another. Store in the refrigerator overnight, mix them together in the morning, and bake.

1. In a medium-size mixing bowl, mix together all the dry ingredients. Add the dried fruit and nuts, the orange rind, and the chopped fresh fruit or berries.
2. In a separate bowl, mix the eggs, honey, milk, vanilla, and butter.
3. Make a well in the center of the dry ingredients. Pour in the wet ingredients, and mix together until well-blended.
4. Butter a muffin tin well—the bottoms and sides of the cups, and the area on the top between muffin cups. Fill each muffin cup as full as you can get it with batter. You will have enough batter for 9–12 muffins. Put the muffin tin on a flat baking tray in case any of the batter spills over.
5. Bake in a preheated 350°F. oven for about 40 minutes, or until the muffins are evenly browned and firm. Lit sit for about 5 minutes to firm up before removing the muffins from the pan.

COCONUT MUFFINS
Substitute 1 cup dried or grated fresh coconut for the nuts in the recipe.

DAN'S OATMEAL MUFFINS
Add 1/2 cup of rolled oats to the batter after it is all mixed. This will make heartier, chewier muffins.

DIN'S POPPYSEED MUFFINS
Mix 1/2 cup of poppyseeds with the milk in a small pot. Simmer over medium heat for about 5 minutes, then add to the wet ingredients as you would plain milk. The poppyseeds give the muffins a nice crunch.

Yield: 9–12 muffins

Grandma's Norwegian Oatmeal Waffles

2 cups milk
2 cups rolled oats
2 eggs, separated
1/3 cup butter, melted
1/3 cup whole wheat pastry flour
1 tablespoon baking powder
1/4 teaspoon salt

Back in the good old days, my grandmother and grandfather ran a Norwegian waffle house in Brooklyn. There were lines around the block waiting to get in. One Christmas my grandparents wanted to go to a big party the relatives were throwing, so they sold the restaurant. I like that story. The oatmeal gives the waffles an extra chewiness.

1. Heat the milk until scalded, then pour it over the rolled oats in a medium-size bowl. Cool for about 30 minutes.
2. Mix in the egg yolks, melted butter, flour, baking powder, and salt.
3. Beat the egg whites until stiff, and fold into the batter.
4. Make the waffles following the directions for your waffle iron. Butter the waffle iron thoroughly, since these waffles are very tender and have a tendency to stick.
5. Serve warm. The traditional accompaniments are butter and homemade jams; butter and maple syrup; and yoghurt, maple syrup, and fresh fruit.

GRANDMA'S OATMEAL PANCAKES
Make the batter exactly as for waffles. Fry the pancakes in butter in a large frying pan, flipping once.

Yield: 4 waffles or 12 pancakes. Serves 4

Desserts

In the past few years I've become aware that there's a place in life for desserts. I used to be preoccupied with the idea of empty calories. When a good friend said, "Isn't cake wonderful!" I reacted with vaguely suppressed disbelief. In the restaurant I rarely made desserts—I let the other cooks do it, occasionally dampening everyone's spirits by mentioning that desserts had lots of calories and very few nutrients.

Why the change of heart? First and foremost I've started to let myself enjoy life more. A good dessert seems to be a genuine treat, an experience of the pure bliss and sweetness of life. I've also started running and can actually feel my body burn up those desserts. As a slightly older and wiser person, I have to agree with my friend Matthew who says, "Don't worry! Eat a wide variety of the best-tasting natural foods you can find, don't eat too much, and exercise."

Through the years we've discovered which types of desserts are the best made with whole wheat flour and honey, and we've worked to perfect those recipes.

If you don't have a baking pan of the size and type recommended in a recipe, substitute the closest sized pan you have. Remember that most desserts expand when baking, so when you're filling a pan, don't push your luck and overfill it. Just bake an extra little pie or cake.

Luscious Coconut Cake

CAKE

3/4 cup unsalted butter, at room
 temperature
2/3 cup honey
2 eggs
2 cups whole wheat pastry flour
1 tablespoon baking powder
1/2 cup milk
1 teaspoon vanilla extract
3/4 cup dried unsweetened or grated fresh
 coconut

CHOCOLATE WHIPPED CREAM
  FROSTING

1 ounce unsweetened baker's chocolate
1/4 cup unsalted butter
1/4 cup honey
1/2 teaspoon vanilla extract
1 cup heavy cream, whipped

Be sure to use unsalted butter so the delicate coconut flavor comes through.

1. In a medium-size mixing bowl, cream the butter until smooth. Mix in the honey, then mix in the eggs 1 at a time.
2. Mix together the flour and baking powder.
3. Mix the milk with the vanilla extract.
4. Add the dry ingredients to the creamed mixture alternately with the milk mixture. Combine lightly after each addition.
5. Mix in the coconut.
6. Pour the batter into a well-buttered 9-inch by 13-inch baking pan. Bake in a preheated 350°F. oven for about 40 minutes, or until the cake is lightly browned and a knife inserted in the center comes out clean. Remove from the oven and allow to cool completely before frosting.
7. To make the frosting, melt the chocolate in a small pot over low heat. In a mixing bowl, beat the butter until smooth. Beat in the honey, then the vanilla extract, then the melted chocolate. Fold in the whipped cream. Spread in a thick layer over the cake.

Yield: One 9-inch by 13-inch cake. Serves 8–12

Amy's Orange Buttercream Torte

TORTE

2/3 cup butter, at room temperature
Grated rind of 1/2 lemon
1/4 cup honey
3 eggs, separated, at room temperature
2 cups whole wheat pastry flour
1 tablespoon baking powder
1/2 cup milk
1 teaspoon vanilla extract or 1/2 teaspoon
   almond extract
1/4 cup honey

ORANGE BUTTERCREAM FILLING

1/4 cup butter
8 ounces cream cheese, at room
   temperature
1/4 cup honey
Grated rind of 1 orange
Juice of 1 orange
1/2 teaspoon vanilla or almond extract
1 1/2 teaspoons arrowroot or cornstarch

TOPPING

1 cup heavy cream

OPTIONAL ADDITIONS

2 tablespoons Grand Marnier
2 tablespoons chopped walnuts or walnut
   pieces

This torte is light and delicate, the filling is creamily orange, and when it's all put together, it looks beautiful. I make this for special dinners and birthday parties.

1. First make the torte. In a medium-size mixing bowl, cream the butter with a wooden spoon until smooth. Add the lemon rind. Add 1/4 cup honey and cream until smooth.
2. Add the egg yolks, 1 at a time, beating well after each addition.
3. Mix together the flour and baking powder. Stir part of this into the butter mixture.
4. Mix together the milk and vanilla. Stir part of this into the butter mixture. Continue alternating additions of flour and milk until all are added.
5. In a separate bowl, beat the egg whites until stiff. Add 1/4 cup honey and beat until as stiff as possible. Fold the egg whites into the cake batter, and continue folding gently until the batter is evenly mixed.
6. Pour the batter into a well-buttered 9-inch or 10-inch cake pan. Bake in a preheated 350°F. oven for about 35 minutes, or until the torte is firm, lightly browned, and a knife inserted in the center comes out clean.
7. Allow to cool for 15 minutes, then remove from the pan.
8. To make the buttercream filling, have all the ingredients measured and ready to go. Melt the butter in a pot over very low heat, or in the top of a double boiler. Still on the heat, mash in the cream cheese with a fork and beat with the fork until smooth. Beat in the honey, orange rind and juice, and vanilla,

until creamy. Beat in the arrowroot or cornstarch. Remove from the heat and allow to cool to room temperature, then refrigerate for about 15 minutes to firm up the filling a little more.

9. In a separate bowl, beat the heavy cream until stiff.

10. To assemble, slice the cake in half horizontally to make 2 layers. For an extra-special flavor, sprinkle the cut edges with Grand Marnier. Spread the buttercream filling on the bottom layer, then cover it with the top layer. Pile the top of the torte with the whipped cream. Decorate with walnuts.

CHOCOLATE ORANGE BUTTERCREAM TORTE

Increase the first addition of honey in the torte batter to 1/2 cup. Mix 1/3 cup of unsweetened cocoa powder in with the flour and the baking powder.

STRAWBERRY SHORTCAKE TORTE

Omit the Orange Buttercream Filling. Slice the torte in half. Fill with whipped cream and sliced strawberries, and top with more strawberries and whipped cream.

Yield: One 9-inch or 10-inch torte. Serves 8

German Chocolate Cake

CAKE

3 ounces unsweetened baker's chocolate
3/4 cup butter, at room temperature
3/4 cup honey
3 eggs, separated
1 1/2 teaspoons vanilla extract
1 1/2 cups whole wheat pastry flour
3/4 teaspoon baking powder
3/4 teaspoon baking soda
1 cup sour cream

COCONUT FROSTING

1/4 cup butter, melted
3/4 cup honey
1/4 cup heavy cream
1/2 cup dried unsweetened or grated fresh
   coconut
1/2 cup chopped walnuts

We cover this rich chocolate cake with a coconut glaze.

1. To prepare the cake first melt the chocolate in a small pot over low heat.
2. In a medium-size mixing bowl, beat the butter until smooth. Beat in the honey, then the melted chocolate. Beat in the egg yolks 1 at a time, then the vanilla.
3. Mix together the flour, baking powder, and baking soda. Add to the chocolate mixture alternately with the sour cream. Mix until well-blended.
4. In a separate bowl, beat the egg whites until stiff. Fold into the batter.
5. Pour the batter into a well-buttered 9-inch by 13-inch baking dish. Bake in a preheated 325°F. oven for 50–60 minutes, until the cake is firm and a knife inserted in the center comes out clean. Be sure the cake is completely baked. If it's not, it will get soggy when you pour the glaze over it.
6. While the cake is baking, prepare the coconut frosting. Melt the butter in a small pot. Mix in the other ingredients.
7. When the cake is done, remove it from the oven, spread with the frosting, and return to the oven to bake for 15 minutes more. The frosting will glaze over the top of the cake.
8. Allow to cool for 30 minutes before serving so the glaze can set.

Yield: One 9-inch by 13-inch cake. Serves 8–12

Cabbagetown Carrot Cake

1 cup honey
1 cup grated raw carrot
1 cup raisins, or combination raisins and chopped dates
1 teaspoon cinnamon
1 teaspoon nutmeg
1/2 teaspoon cloves
1/2 cup butter
1 cup water
2 cups whole wheat pastry flour
2 teaspoons baking soda
3/4 cup coarsely chopped walnuts or hazelnuts

A young woman appeared from some Cornell or Ithaca program for "a day in the kitchen." Then she disappeared, leaving us with this very moist and tender carrot cake recipe. This recipe multiplies nicely for large sheet cakes. We've used it for several weddings.

1. In a medium-size pot combine the honey, carrot, raisins, spices, butter, and water. Bring to a boil and boil for 5 minutes, stirring frequently. Remove from the heat and allow to cool to lukewarm, about 45 minutes.

2. Measure the flour into a mixing bowl. Rub the baking soda between your hands to remove any lumps, and mix into the flour along with the nuts.

3. Make a well in the center of the flour mixture and pour in the cooled carrot mixture. Mix the dry and wet ingredients together thoroughly.

4. Pour into a well-buttered 10-inch springform pan or any equivalent-size pans.

5. Bake in a preheated 325°F. oven for 40 minutes, or until the cake is lightly browned, firm, and a knife inserted in the center comes out clean.

6. Allow to cool for 15 minutes before removing from the pan. Serve warm, if possible, with whipped cream or vanilla ice cream. Or cool the cake and frost it with Cream Cheese Frosting (page 207).

Yield: One 10-inch cake. Serves 8

Johnny Appleseed Cake

1 1/2 cups applesauce or 3–4 apples, diced
2 cups whole wheat pastry flour
1 teaspoon cinnamon
1/2 teaspoon nutmeg
1/4 teaspoon cloves
1 cup raisins
1 cup coarsely chopped walnuts
1/2 cup butter
2/3 cup honey
2 teaspoons baking soda

This light spice cake is what my mother makes for me on my birthday. I am famous for eating the whole cake by myself on my birthday my freshman year in college. The story isn't true since I did share a piece with my friend next door. You start with applesauce or with fresh apples and make them into applesauce.

1. If you are using fresh apples, put them in a medium-size pot with 2 tablespoons of water. Simmer covered for about 30 minutes, or until the apples have become hot, thick applesauce. Measure out 1 1/2 cups and return to the pot to keep it warm. If you are using applesauce, put it in a saucepan and warm it over low heat.
2. Mix together the flour, spices, raisins, and walnuts in a mixing bowl.
3. Melt the butter in a small pot and mix in the honey. Stir into the dry ingredients.
4. Stir the baking soda into the hot applesauce in the pot. This will foam up in a spectacular fashion. Add to the batter in the bowl and mix thoroughly.
5. Pour the batter into a well-buttered 9-inch square cake pan.
6. Bake in a preheated 325°F. oven for about 40 minutes, or until a knife inserted in the center comes out clean.
7. Serve warm with vanilla ice cream or cool and frost with Cream Cheese Frosting (page 207).

Yield: One 9-inch square cake. Serves 8

Cream Cheese Frosting

8 ounces cream cheese, at room
    temperature
1/4 cup butter, at room temperature
1/4 honey or maple syrup
1/2 teaspoon vanilla extract or 1/4
    teaspoon almond extract
Grated rind of 1/2 lemon or 1/2 orange
2 tablespoons heavy cream

Here's the white natural foods frosting. It has a good flavor and a light consistency if you whip it up well.

1. Beat together the cream cheese and butter. It is important that you beat this mixture until it is completely smooth, or your frosting will have lumps.
2. Beat in the honey, then the vanilla and lemon rind, then the cream, a little bit at a time. Continue beating until the icing is smooth and creamy.
3. Taste and add anything you want to make the frosting completely delicious—a little more lemon rind, a little grand Marnier, whatever.

NUTTY CREAM CHEESE FROSTING:
Add 1/2 cup chopped walnuts and 1/2 cup coconut.

Yield: Frosting for one 9-inch or 10-inch cake

Grandma's Sour Cream Coffee Cake

CAKE

1/2 cup butter, at room temperature
2/3 cup honey
2 eggs
1 teaspoon vanilla extract
2 cups whole wheat pastry flour
1 teaspoon baking powder
1 teaspoon baking soda
1 cup sour cream

FILLING

3/4 cup chopped walnuts
1/3 cup honey
1 teaspoon cinnamon

This rich coffee cake has a cinnamon walnut filling.

1. In a medium-size mixing bowl, cream the butter and honey until smooth. Add the eggs, 1 at a time, and beat well. Beat in the vanilla.
2. Mix together the dry ingredients. Add to the batter alternately with the sour cream, until all is well-mixed.
3. Mix together the filling ingredients in a small bowl.
4. Butter a tube pan or a 9-inch square cake pan. Put in half the batter. Sprinkle with half the nut mixture. Add the remaining batter and top with the rest of the nut mixture.
5. Bake in a preheated 350°F. oven for about 45 minutes, or until the cake is firm and lightly browned and a knife inserted in the center comes out clean.

BLUEBERRY COFFEE CAKE
Mix 1 cup fresh or frozen blueberries into the cake batter.

CRANBERRY COFFEE CAKE
Mix 1 cup fresh or frozen cranberries and the grated rind of 1 orange into the cake batter.

Yield: One tube. Serves 8

Rhubarb Kuchen

SHELL

1 1/2 cups whole wheat pastry flour
Grated rind of 1 lemon
1/2 teaspoon baking powder
1/2 cup cold butter
1/4 cup honey
1 egg
1 teaspoon vanilla extract

FILLING

4 cups chopped rhubarb
2 egg yolks
1 cup sour cream
1/2 cup honey
1 teaspoon vanilla extract
2 tablespoons whole wheat pastry flour

TOPPING

2 egg whites
Honey

A pastry crust, a luscious fruit filling, and a meringue top make this a real knock-out, a good dessert for company.

1. To make the shell, mix the flour with the lemon rind and baking powder. Grate in the butter and mix. Mix in the honey, egg, and vanilla. Pat the dough onto the bottom of a well-buttered 10-inch springform pan. Make a small lip around the sides of the pan.
2. Mix together the ingredients of the filling in a mixing bowl. Pour into the shell. Bake in a preheated 350°F. oven for 50–60 minutes, until firm.
3. Beat the 2 egg whites with a tiny bit of honey until stiff. Spread over the cake, being sure to bring the meringue to the edge of the pan to prevent shrinking. Return to the oven and bake until lightly browned, about 5 minutes.
4. Allow to cool in the pan for 30 minutes to firm up thoroughly. To serve remove from the pan onto a nice serving plate.

STRAWBERRY RHUBARB KUCHEN
It's delicious. Substitute 2 cups sliced strawberries for 2 cups of the rhubarb.

FRESH FRUIT KUCHEN
Substitute 4 cups sliced apples or peaches or pitted sour cherries for the rhubarb.

Yield: One 10-inch cake. Serves 8

Anne's Fresh Fruit Tart

PASTRY SHELL

3 egg whites
1 teaspoon fresh lemon juice
Pinch salt
2 teaspoons honey
1 1/4 cups whole wheat pastry flour
1/2 cup cold unsalted butter

PASTRY CREAM

1 cup heavy cream
1/4 cup honey
3 egg yolks
Pinch salt
3 tablespoons whole wheat pastry flour
1/2 teaspoon vanilla extract
1/2 tablespoon unsalted butter

TOP LAYERS

1/2 teaspoon kirsch or cognac (optional)
3 tablespoons jam
1/3 cup cake or bread crumbs
About 2 cups fresh fruit slices

This dessert is a little complicated, but it's worth the work. Anne had an amazing ability to make French desserts during the most frantic and chaotic cooking shifts. We'd turn around and a masterpiece would be sitting on the back counter. "Use beautiful sliced fresh fruits," says Anne. "Bananas, apples, and pears are not ideal because they turn brown too fast. Grapes are great. Strawberries, oranges, cantaloupe, honeydew, kiwis, and mangos are wonderful!"

1. First make the pastry shell. Combine the egg whites, lemon juice, salt, and honey. Beat well with a fork.
2. Measure the flour into a separate bowl. Grate in the butter and rub it with your fingertips until it resembles coarse sand in texture.
3. Stir in the egg mixture to make a soft dough. Turn the dough onto a large sheet of waxed paper and flatten it with a rolling pin to a rectangle about 8 inches by 4 inches. Cover with another sheet of waxed paper, and refrigerate for at least 30 minutes.
4. Using a rolling pin, roll the dough out between the waxed paper to a rectangle about 14 inches by 7 inches. Cutting through the paper, trim to 12 inches by 5 inches, saving the trimmings. Dampen a baking sheet by rubbing it with a little water. Peel off the paper and turn the dough onto the baking sheet. Use the dough trimmings to make a raised rim all around the rectangular shell.
5. Prick with a fork. Refrigerate for about 15 minutes.

6. Bake in a preheated 350°F. oven for 15–18 minutes, until it is lightly browned. Chill it thoroughly on the baking sheet.

7. To make the pastry cream, combine 3/4 cup of the cream with the honey in a small saucepan and heat over low heat to simmering. Remove from the heat.

8. In another saucepan, not yet on the heat, whisk the egg yolks and salt. Add the remaining 1/4 cup cream. Whisk in the flour until smooth. Slowly pour in the hot cream mixture, whisking vigorously.

9. Place on low heat, whisking until the mixture is a thick pudding. Remove from the heat. Add the vanilla and dot with the butter. Cool.

10. To assemble the tart, stir the liquor into the jam in a saucepan. Melt and remove from the heat. Brush the warm jam onto the pastry, excluding the rim.

11. Sprinkle with the cake or bread crumbs.

12. Spoon dollops of pastry cream over the tart. Spread it carcfully to keep the crumbs from mixing into it. Cover the tart shell except for the rim.

13. Arrange the fruits in rows. Chill.

14. When you're ready to serve it, remove the tart very carefully from the baking sheet using 2 long spatulas. Take care because the pastry is brittle. Transfer it to a serving tray or a good-looking wooden cutting board.

Yield: Serves 6

Rhubarb Custard Pie

9-inch or 10-inch Whole Wheat Pie Crusts
  (page 132)
4 cups chopped rhubarb
3/4 cup honey
3 tablespoons whole wheat pastry flour
1/4 teaspoon nutmeg
Juice of 1 orange
1 egg
2 tablespoons butter

The first fresh fruit pie of the year. This is particularly welcome on a cold April day.

1. Follow the pie crust recipe to make dough for 9 or 10-inch bottom and top crusts. Roll out half the pie dough for your bottom crust, and fit it into a well-buttered 9-inch or 10-inch pie pan. Roll out the other half of the dough as a flat round about 2 inches wider than the top of the pie pan. Set aside.
2. Mix together the rhubarb, honey, flour, nutmeg, orange juice, and egg in a mixing bowl.
3. Pour the filling into the prepared pie shell. Dot with butter.
4. To make a lattice top, cut the flat round of pie crust into 8 strips about 3/4 inch wide. Lay 4 of them parallel across the top of the pie. Then weave the other 4 pieces, 1 at a time, through the base pieces. Start them alternately on the top and on the bottom, so you have a real weaving. Pinch the edges of the lattice together with the bottom crust. Then merge them by fluting the rim of the crust.
5. Bake in a preheated 350°F. oven for about 50 minutes, or until the lattice crust is lightly browned and the filling is bubbly.

STRAWBERRY RHUBARB CUSTARD PIE
Substitute 2 cups sliced fresh strawberries for 2 cups of rhubarb. Decrease the honey to 1/2 cup.

Yield: One 9-inch or 10-inch pie. Serves 6–8

Apple Pie

9-inch or 10-inch Whole Wheat Pie Crusts (page 132)
6 cups sliced apples
Juice of 1/2 lemon
1/4 cup honey
1/4 cup whole wheat pastry flour
1/2 teaspoon cinnamon
2 tablespoons butter

We leave the skins on when we slice the apples.

1. Follow the pie crust recipe to make dough for 9 or 10-inch bottom and top crusts. Roll out half the dough for your bottom crust, and fit it into a well-buttered 9-inch or 10-inch pie pan. Roll out the other half of the dough as a flat round about 2 inches wider than the top of the pie pan. Set aside.
2. Mix together the sliced apples, lemon juice, honey, pastry flour, and cinnamon in a mixing bowl.
3. Pour the filling into the pie shell. Dot with butter.
4. Place the top crust over the pie, press the rims together, turn them under, and flute for decoration. Slash the top of the pie with an "A" or with a design to let the steam escape.
5. Bake in a preheated 350°F. oven for 45–50 minutes, until the crust is golden brown and the filling looks delicious and bubbly.
6. Serve warm, plain, with vanilla or lemon cinnamon ice cream, or with Cheddar cheese.

APPLE CRANBERRY PIE
Use 2 cups cranberries and 4 cups sliced apples. Increase the honey to 1/3 cup.

FRESH FRUIT PIE
Instead of apples use cherries, blueberries, peaches, pears, plums, or any combination of fruits you like.

Yield: One 9-inch or 10-inch pie. Serves 6–8

Apple Crisp

FRUIT

8 cups sliced apples
Juice of 1 lemon
1 teaspoon cinnamon
1/2 teaspoon nutmeg
1/4 cup cold butter, grated
1/2 cup honey

TOPPING

3 cups rolled oats
2 cups whole wheat pastry flour
1/2 teaspoon baking powder
1 cup cold butter, grated
1/2 cup honey
1/2 teaspoon vanilla extract

You can make a crisp with any fruit or fruit combination that's in season, or you can use frozen fruits in the winter. Cabbagetown's crisp topping is especially good.

1. Mix together the fruit ingredients to make the filling. Pat the mixture into a well-buttered 9-inch by 13-inch baking dish.
2. In a medium-size bowl, mix together the topping ingredients with your fingers. Crumble the topping over the fruit mixture.
3. Bake in a preheated 350°F. oven for 45–60 minutes, until the crisp topping is evenly golden brown. Since some ovens bake unevenly, it's a good idea to check the crisp and turn the pan around after 30 minutes.
4. Serve while still warm if possible. Fruit crisps are great alone, but even more sumptuous with vanilla ice cream on top.

APPLE-RHUBARB CRISP

Use 4 cups sliced apples and 4 cups chopped rhubarb in the filling. Increase the honey to 3/4 cup.

APPLE-STRAWBERRY CRISP

Use 4 cups sliced strawberries and 4 cups sliced apples.

BLACK RASPBERRY, RED RASPBERRY, OR BLACKBERRY CRISP

Use 8 cups of berries in the filling.

CHERRY CRISP

Use 8 cups sweet or sour pitted cherries. For the sour cherries increase the honey to 3/4 cup.

PEACH CRISP

Use 8 cups sliced peaches.

BLUEBERRY CRISP

Use 8 cups blueberries.

PEAR CRISP

Use 8 cups sliced pears.

APPLE-CRANBERRY CRISP

Use 4 cups sliced apples and 4 cups cranberries in the filling. Increase the honey to 3/4 cup.

Yield: One 9-inch by 13-inch pan. Serves 8

Julie and runner friends who joyfully tasted every recipe in the book and gave opinions

Peach Crumble Pie Deluxe

BOTTOM CRUST

**9-inch or 10-inch Whole Wheat Pie Crust
(page 132)**

FILLING

**6 cups sliced peaches
Juice of 1/2 lemon
1/4 cup honey
1/4 cup whole wheat pastry flour
2 tablespoons butter**

SOUR CREAM LAYER

**2 cups sour cream
1 tablespoon honey
2 teaspoons cinnamon**

CRUMBLE TOPPING

**1 1/2 cups rolled oats
1 cup whole wheat pastry flour
1/2 cup chopped walnuts
1/2 cup cold butter, grated
1/4 cup honey
1/2 teaspoon vanilla extract**

This pie has brought more proposals of marriage to the Cabbagetown cooks than everything else we serve in the restaurant combined.

1. First prepare the bottom crust, following the recipe to make 1 bottom crust. Roll out and fit it into a well-buttered 9-inch or 10-inch pie pan. Flute the rim.
2. In a medium-size mixing bowl, mix together the filling ingredients.
3. In another bowl, mix together the ingredients for the sour cream layer.
4. In a third bowl, mix together the topping ingredients. Mix with your fingers until well-blended.
5. Pour the peaches into the bottom crust. Smooth the sour cream over that. Finally pat the topping over it all.
6. Bake in a preheated 350°F. oven for 45–50 minutes, until the crumble topping is evenly golden brown.
7. Serve warm if possible.

PEACH-RASPBERRY CRUMBLE PIE DELUXE
Substitute 2 cups red raspberries for 2 cups of the peaches.

PEAR CRUMBLE PIE DELUXE
Pears make a delicious late fall pie. Substitute 6 cups sliced pears for the peaches.

Yield: One 9-inch or 10-inch pie. Serves 6–8

Betsy's Blueberry Cobbler

FRUIT

4 cups blueberries
Juice of 1/2 lemon
1/2 teaspoon cinnamon
1/4 cup honey
3 tablespoons cold butter, grated

TOPPING

5 tablespoons butter
1/2 cup honey
1 egg
1 cup whole wheat pastry flour
1 1/2 teaspoons baking powder
1/4 teaspoon cinnamon
1/4 cup milk

Betsy's quick and simple cobbler recipe is a good way to serve any juicy fruit or berry. Plan to make it shortly before you want to serve it, so the cobbler is still warm.

1. Mix together the blueberries, lemon juice, cinnamon, honey, and butter. Pat the fruit mixture into a well-buttered 9-inch square baking pan or a 10-inch round pan.
2. To make the topping, cream 5 tablespoons butter with 1/2 cup honey. Beat in the egg. Mix together the dry ingredients. Add to the creamed mixture alternately with the milk.
3. Spread the topping as smoothly as possible over the fruit.
4. Bake in a preheated 325°F. oven for 40–45 minutes, until the cobbler is lightly browned and a knife inserted in the center comes out clean. Do not overbake or the cobbler will be tough.
5. Serve plain or with vanilla ice cream.

STRAWBERRY RHUBARB COBBLER
Use 2 cups chopped rhubarb and 2 cups sliced strawberries.

BERRY OR CHERRY COBBLER
Use 4 cups any berry or combination of berries.

PEACH COBBLER
Use 4 cups sliced peaches.

Yield: One 9-inch square or 10-inch round pan. Serves 6

Ådel's Cranberry Walnut Pie

9-inch or 10-inch Whole Wheat Pie Crust
  (page 132)
3/4 cup coarsely chopped walnuts
3 eggs
3/4 cup combination milk and heavy cream
1/2 cup maple syrup
2 cups fresh or frozen cranberries

Ådel's cooking is Norway's gift to Cabbagetown.

1. First prepare the crust, following the recipe to make 1 bottom crust. Roll out and fit it into a well-buttered 9-inch or 10-inch pie pan. Flute the rim.
2. Sprinkle the chopped nuts in the crust.
3. In a medium-size mixing bowl, whisk together the eggs, milk, and maple syrup. Pour over the nuts.
4. Sprinkle the cranberries over the top of the pie.
5. Bake in a preheated 350°F. oven until the custard in the center of the pie is firm, about 45 minutes.
6. Allow to settle for at least 20 minutes before serving, so the texture can firm and the pie can cool to its best flavor. Then serve the pie warm or chill it and serve it cold.

Yield: One 9-inch or 10-inch pie. Serves 6

June's Two Crust Pumpkin Pie

9-inch or 10-inch Whole Wheat Pie Crusts
  (page 132)
6 cups raw pumpkin cubes (Start with a
  2–3 pound pumpkin.)
1/2 cup honey
1 teaspoon cinnamon
5 tablespoons whole wheat pastry flour
2 tablespoons butter

This is an unusual variation on pumpkin pie. You treat the pumpkin like apples, cube it, and bake it with a top crust.

1. Prepare the pie dough according to the recipe and roll out half the dough for a bottom crust. Fit it into a well-buttered 9-inch or 10-inch pie pan. Roll out the other half of the dough as a flat round about 2 inches wider than the top of the pie pan. Set aside.
2. Peel and core the pumpkin. Dice into 1/4-inch cubes.
3. Mix the pumpkin cubes with the honey, cinnamon, and pastry flour. Pour into the prepared pie shell and dot with butter.
4. Place the top crust over the pie, press the rims together, turn them under, and flute for decoration. Slash the top of the pie to let steam escape.
5. Bake in a preheated 350°F. oven for 1 hour or slightly more, until the top crust is lightly browned.
6. This pie is especially good served warm from the oven with vanilla ice cream.

TWO-CRUST SQUASH PIE
Use winter squash (butternut, acorn, hubbard) instead of the pumpkin. Since squash is less watery than pumpkin, decrease the whole wheat flour in the filling to 3 tablespoons.

Yield: One 9-inch or 10-inch pie. Serves 6–8

Homemade Graham Cracker Crusts

4 cups whole wheat pastry flour
1 teaspoon cinnamon
1 cup cold butter
1/2 cup honey
1/2 cup cold butter
1/4 cup honey or maple syrup

To make graham cracker crusts from scratch, first you make a huge graham cracker, then you break that up and make it into pie crusts. One taste will convince you it's worth it. As with regular pie crusts, I always recommend making 2 crusts at once. You can use one and freeze the other.

1. Measure the flour and cinnamon into a medium-size mixing bowl. Grate in 1 cup cold butter. Add 1/2 cup honey, and rub it all between your hands until it is well-mixed.
2. Butter a cookie sheet. Pat the crumb mixture out flat on the cookie sheet, making sure the edges are as thick as the middle so they don't brown too quickly.
3. Bake in a preheated 350°F. oven for 20–25 minutes, until it's lightly browned all over. Allow to cool.
4. Take this graham cracker, and depending on how hard it is, either crumble it with your hands, or beat it with a rolling pin until you have fine crumbs.
5. Put the crumbs into a bowl. Grate in the remaining 1/2 cup butter, add the remaining 1/4 cup honey or maple syrup, and mix it with your hands until it holds together.
6. Butter two 9-inch or 10-inch pie pans. Pat half the crumbs into each pan, pressing the crumbs into the pans first on the sides and then on the bottoms.
7. Bake in a preheated 350°F. oven for about 10 minutes to firm the crusts.
8. Fill 'em up!

Yield: Two 10-inch dessert pie crusts

Sharon's Pumpkin Pie

9-inch or 10-inch Whole Wheat Pie Crust (page 132) or Graham Cracker Crust (page 221)
2 cups pumpkin purée (Start with a 2–3 pound pumpkin.)
2 eggs
1/2 cup honey
1 cup heavy cream or sour cream
1/2 cup milk
1 teaspoon cinnamon
1/2 teaspoon ginger
1/2 teaspoon cloves
1/4 teaspoon salt

1. First prepare a bottom pastry or graham cracker pie crust, and fit it into a well-buttered 9-inch or 10-inch pie pan. Flute the rim of a pastry crust.

2. We have 2 ways of preparing pumpkin purée from raw pumpkin. You can cut your pumpkin in half, core it, and put it face-down in a baking pan with 1/2 inch of water. Bake in a 350°F. oven for about 1 hour or until tender. Then scoop out the pulp. Mash it with a fork just enough to measure it, and measure out 2 cups. The faster way to prepare the purée is to peel and core the pumpkin. Cut it into large pieces. Put them in a medium-size pot with 1/2 inch of water. Bring to a boil, then reduce the heat and simmer, covered, for 15–20 minutes, until the pumpkin is tender when pierced with a fork. Mash with a fork just enough to measure it, and measure out 2 cups. (Extra cooked pumpkin can be frozen for future pies.)

3. Put the pumpkin and all other ingredients in the blender and blend until smooth.

4. Pour into the prepared pie shell. Don't overfill it, or it will just run over in the oven. Pour extra pie filling into a small well-buttered baking dish and bake it to make pumpkin custard.

5. Bake in a preheated 350°F. oven for about 1 hour, or until the pie is firm and a knife inserted in the center comes out clean.

6. Allow to settle for about 20 minutes before serving to firm the textures.

SQUASH PIE OR SWEET POTATO PIE

Prepare winter squash or sweet potato purée the same way you would prepare pumpkin purée. These pies are just like pumpkin pie but more richly flavored.

Yield: One 9-inch or 10-inch pie, plus some extra pumpkin custard. Serves 6–8

Sharon

Sour Cream Cheese Pie

CRUST

**9-inch or 10-inch Graham Cracker Crust
(page 221)**

CREAM CHEESE LAYER

**8 ounces cream cheese, at room
temperature**
1/4 cup honey
2 eggs
1/2 teaspoon vanilla extract
Juice of 1/2 lemon

SOUR CREAM LAYER

2 cups sour cream
3 tablespoons honey
1/2 teaspoon vanilla extract
Pinch cinnamon

Every restaurant I've worked in has had a recipe similar to this one. It's always a hit. The honey version has a little lemon in it for freshness.

1. First prepare the crust.
2. In a medium-size bowl, beat the cream cheese until smooth with a wooden spoon. Beat in 1/4 cup honey. Beat in the eggs, 1 at a time, then the 1/2 teaspoon vanilla and lemon juice. Pour into the prepared crust. Bake in a preheated 350°F. oven for about 20 minutes or until firm.
3. Mix the sour cream, 3 tablespoons honey, 1/2 teaspoon vanilla, and cinnamon. Spread on the pie. Return to the oven and bake for about 10 minutes, until set. Or return to the oven, turn off the heat, and allow the pie to bake slowly for about 20 minutes, until set.
4. Cool, then chill thoroughly before serving to firm the textures.

FRESH BERRY CREAM CHEESE PIE
After the pie is cooled, cover the top with sliced fresh strawberries, red raspberries, sweet cherries, or blueberries.

Yield: One 9-inch or 10-inch pie. Serves 6–8

Ellen's Pineapple Cheesecake

CRUST
1 cup whole wheat pastry flour
1 cup chopped walnuts
1 cup cold butter
1/2 cup honey

FILLING
1 1/2 pounds cream cheese, at room temperature
5 eggs, separated
2/3 cup maple syrup
1 1/2 teaspoons vanilla
1 tablespoon arrowroot or cornstarch

TOPPING
2 cups finely chopped fresh ripe pineapple

1. First prepare the crust. In a medium-size mixing bowl, mix the flour with the chopped nuts. Grate in the butter. Mix in with your fingers. Mix in the honey with your fingers. Pat onto the bottom of a 10-inch springform pan. Bake in a preheated 325°F. oven for 15 minutes.

2. Meanwhile prepare the filling. In a medium-size mixing bowl, beat the cream cheese until smooth. Beat in the egg yolks 1 at a time. It is important that you beat these until the mixture is smooth so there will be no lumps in the cake. Beat in the maple syrup, then the vanilla, then the arrowroot or cornstarch.

3. In a separate bowl, beat the egg whites until stiff. Fold into the batter.

4. Pour the filling into the crust and return to the 325 degreesF. oven. Bake for about 1 hour or until the cheesecake is just firm. Don't overbake or it will be tough.

5. Cool completely before unspringing the cake from the pan, then chill in the refrigerator. Before serving, cover the top with chopped fresh pineapple. Cut with a knife dipped in hot water.

ELLEN'S CHOCOLATE SWIRL CHEESECAKE
Melt 2 ounces unsweetened baker's chocolate. Mix in 1/2 cup maple syrup. Pour this over the cheesecake filling in the crust, and swirl it in with a chopstick.

Yield: One 10-inch cheesecake. Serves 8–12

Stina's Cottage Cheese Bun Pie

BUN DOUGH

1/2 cup hot water
2 tablespoons honey
1 teaspoon active dry yeast
1/4 cup dried milk powder
Grated rind of 1/4 lemon
1/4 teaspoon ground cardamon
2 tablespoons butter, melted
1–1 1/4 cups whole wheat bread flour
Heavy cream (optional)

FILLING

2 cups cottage cheese
1/3 cup honey
1/2 cup almonds, finely chopped
1/4 teaspoon almond extract
2 teaspoons vanilla extract
Grated rind of 1/2 lemon
1/4 cup raisins

You feel healthy when you eat this light Swedish cheesecake. I like it as a dessert, as a coffee cake, and as a breakfast cake. The crust is a sweet yeast dough.

1. In a medium-size mixing bowl, dissolve the honey in the hot water. While it is still warm, drop in the yeast. Let it sit for 5–10 minutes while the yeast bubbles up. Then stir in the milk powder, lemon rind, cardamon, and melted butter. Stir in about 1 cup flour, enough to make a loose dough. Allow to rise in a warm spot for 1 hour.
2. Meanwhile prepare the filling. Rub the cottage cheese through a strainer to get it smooth. This may seem like a lot of work, but do it! If you don't, your filling will be grainy and runny rather than smooth. Mix the cottage cheese together with the remaining ingredients in a medium-size mixing bowl. Set aside.
3. Butter a 9-inch or 10-inch pie pan.
4. Turn the dough onto a floured counter, and knead until it holds together in a ball, adding more flour if necessary. Roll out the dough with a rolling pin until it fits neatly in the bottom and sides of the pie pan. Add the filling. For a nice touch, paint the edges of the crust with heavy cream.
5. Bake in a preheated 350°F. oven for 25–30 minutes, until the crust is lightly browned and the filling is firm.
6. Allow to settle for at least 30 minutes before serving to firm the textures.

Yield: One 9-inch or 10-inch pie. Serves 6

Din's New England Bread Pudding

3 cups bread, broken in pieces the size of
  your thumbnail
1/2 cup raisins
3 cups milk
1/4 cup butter
3 eggs
1/3 cup honey or maple syrup
1 teaspoon cinnamon
1/4 teaspoon nutmeg
1 teaspoon vanilla extract

One day when Din made her bread pudding for lunch, an elderly gentleman who had just been served a dish of it stood up in the middle of the crowded dining room. "I just want you all to know," he boomed, "that I have traveled all around the world eating bread pudding, and this is the best I've had anywhere." Bread pudding is a good way to use old bread, but it's delicious enough to make from fresh bread if you have the urge.

1. Butter a 2-quart baking dish. In it sprinkle the bread pieces and raisins in loose layers. Don't pack them down.
2. In a medium-size pot, heat the milk until it's warm. Add the butter and continue heating until the butter is melted.
3. In a mixing bowl, beat the eggs. Beat in the honey or maple syrup, then the milk and butter mixture, then the spices and vanilla. Pour over the bread in the baking dish.
4. Bake in a preheated 350°F. oven for about 40 minutes, until the pudding is firm, lightly browned, and a knife inserted in the center comes out clean.
5. Allow to settle for about 15 minutes before serving. Then serve it warm with whipped cream or vanilla ice cream.

APPLE BREAD PUDDING
Mixed 2 diced apples in with the bread and raisins.

Yield: 2-quart baking dish. Serves 6–8

Fresh Strawberry Mousse

1/2 cup honey
2 cups sliced fresh strawberries
15–16 ounces ricotta (about 2 cups)
1/2 teaspoon vanilla extract
1/2 cup heavy cream

Nothing could be simpler than this delicious and refreshing dessert. You can make this with many different berries and fresh fruits through the season, or with frozen fruits in the winter.

1. If your honey has crystallized, heat it until it is liquid.
2. Measure all the ingredients into the blender and blend until smooth. Taste.
3. Pour into serving glasses and chill.

FRESH FRUIT MOUSSE
Apricots, peaches, and raspberries are all delicious when substituted for the strawberries. Blend in a banana for extra richness.

Yield: Serves 6

NOTE: If you are using very juicy strawberries, blend the mixture first, omitting the heavy cream. Then add the heavy cream to the point where you have a smooth, mousse-like mixture. You want your blended mousse to be thick not soupy.

Carob Mousse

1/2 cup honey
1/2 cup carob powder
1/2 teaspoon vanilla extract
1/2 cup milk
1/2 cup heavy cream
15–16 ounces ricotta (about 2 cups)
1 cup heavy cream, whipped

This is a very rich instant dessert.

1. Heat the honey gently in a small pot until it is liquid and warm. Stir the carob into the honey until smooth.
2. Pour into the blender, along with the vanilla, milk, cream, and ricotta. Blend until smooth. Taste.
3. Serve chilled, topped with whipped cream. Or spoon it into parfait glasses in alternate layers with whipped cream, then chill.

Yield: Serves 6

Leche Clema

2 cups milk
1/3 cup whole wheat pastry flour
1/3 cup maple syrup
2 eggs, separated
1 cup heavy cream, whipped

This light pudding sweetened with maple syrup is a good dessert with Mexican meals. We adapted it from Arturo de Don Peralta, who runs an excellent restaurant in Taos, New Mexico.

1. Mix the milk, flour, and maple syrup in a medium-size pot, and simmer until the mixture is like a thin pudding, about 15 minutes. Stir constantly to prevent lumps from forming.
2. In a separate bowl, beat the egg yolks. Beat in a little of the milk mixture, then add back to the main mixture.
3. Beat the egg whites until stiff. Fold in.
4. Chill thoroughly, and serve topped with whipped cream.

Yield: Serves 6

Zabaione

4 **egg yolks**
1 **tablespoon maple syrup**
1/2 **cup dry or cream sherry**
1 **cup sliced fresh strawberries, raspberries,**
   peaches or blueberries
1/2 **cup heavy cream, whipped**

This voluptuous custard can be made in minutes right before serving.

1. In a medium-size heavy pot, whisk the egg yolks and maple syrup for 2–3 minutes, until frothy, fluffy, and pale yellow.
2. Stir in the sherry and put over low heat. Cook, whisking constantly, until the custard thickens. Be careful. This happens very fast, in about 1 minute. Don't let the mixture boil or it will curdle.
3. Pour the warm custard into 4 parfait glasses or small serving bowls. Sprinkle with fresh fruit and top with whipped cream. Serve immediately.

Yield: Serves 4

Carob Brownies

1 cup butter
1 cup carob powder
2/3 cup honey
4 eggs, separated
1 teaspoon vanilla extract
1 cup chopped almonds or walnuts
1/3 cup whole wheat pastry flour
1 teaspoon baking powder

You can truly love these and not even think of chocolate.

1. Melt the butter in a medium-size pot. Remove from the heat. Stir in the carob. Then mix in the honey, egg yolks, vanilla, and nuts.
2. Mix together the flour and baking powder and stir into the wet ingredients.
3. Beat the egg whites until stiff. Fold into the batter.
4. Pour into a well-buttered 9-inch square pan.
5. Bake in a preheated 350°F. oven for about 40 minutes, or until the brownies are firm.
6. Serve immediately while still warm, or cool in the pan before cutting and serving.

Yield: 9 brownies

Date Nut Bars

1/4 cup butter
1/2 cup maple syrup
2 eggs, lightly beaten
2 cups coarsely chopped dates
1 cup coarsely chopped walnuts
1/2 cup plus 1 tablespoon whole wheat
    pastry flour
1/2 teaspoon baking powder

These bars are chewy and sweet.

1. In a medium-size pot, melt the butter. Remove from the heat. Mix in the maple syrup, and as soon as the mixture has cooled a little, mix in the eggs. Add the dates and walnuts.
2. Combine the flour and baking powder and add to the mixture in the pot.
3. Pour the batter into a well-buttered 9-inch square baking pan. Bake in a preheated 350°F. oven for 45–50 minutes, or until the center is firm.
4. When cool, cut into bars.

Yield: 24 bars

Maple Lace Cookies

1/2 cup butter
2 cups rolled oats
3/4 cup maple syrup
1 teaspoon vanilla extract
1/4 teaspoon salt
1 teaspoon baking soda
1 1/2 cups whole wheat pastry flour

I received more letters about this cookie than about any other recipe in *Wings of Life*. Whether the cookies lace out or not depends on exactly what kind of flour and what kind of rolled oats you are using. If you make these cookies once and they don't spread out, make them with less flour the next time.

1. In a medium-size mixing bowl, beat the butter until smooth. Beat in the oats, then the maple syrup, then the vanilla.
2. Stir in the salt, then the baking soda, then the flour. Stir until smooth.
3. Drop the batter by teaspoonfuls onto a buttered cookie sheet. Leave the cookies room to spread out. Bake in a preheated 325°F. oven for about 15 minutes or until the cookies are firm. Let the cookies cool for a few minutes on the baking sheets before you remove them. Lace cookies have a very fragile texture.

Yield: 36 cookies

Joe's Famous Cookies

1/2 cup butter, at room temperature
1 cup peanut butter ("Crunchy," says Joe)
1/2 cup honey or maple syrup
1 egg
1 teaspoon vanilla extract
1 1/2 cups whole wheat pastry flour
1/2 cup rolled oats
1/2 teaspoon baking soda
1 cup carob chips or 1 cup "non-natural chocolate chips sweetened with white sugar"

Joe is a student of ancient history who worked at Cabbagetown for a year. This recipe is as he gave it.

1. Mash up the butter and peanut butter until creamy. Add the honey or maple syrup and stir thoroughly. Mix in the egg until it is indiscernible in the batter. Mix in the vanilla. Stir well.
2. Combine the dry ingredients. Stir into the wet ingredients until well-mixed.
3. Fold in the chips.
4. Drop the batter by teaspoonfuls onto a buttered cookie sheet. Bake in a preheated 350°F. oven for about 30 minutes, until lightly browned. (You can keep this batter in the refrigerator and bake the cookies just a few at a time in the toaster oven, whenever you need cookies for happiness.)

WALNUT & RAISIN COOKIES
All obvious good and wonderful things can be added to the recipe, especially raisins and walnuts.

CHEESECAKE COOKIES
Spread half the cookie dough on the bottom of a 9-inch square pan. Mix together 8 ounces cream cheese, 1/3 cup honey, and 1 egg. Spread over the cookie dough. Top with the remaining cookie dough. Bake in a 350°F. oven for about 40 minutes, until light brown and firm.

Yield: 18–24 cookies

Honey Vanilla Ice Cream

CUSTARD

3 cups milk or half-and-half
1 cup honey or maple syrup
5 eggs
2 cups heavy cream
1 tablespoon vanilla extract

FOR FREEZING

4 or 5 quart ice cream freezer
Ice or snow
Salt or rock salt
Water

One week the quote on the Cabbagetown blackboard was, "Without ice cream, the world would be darkness and chaos." We immediately got into trouble because the customers pointed out that we don't serve ice cream in the restaurant. (I regret that we don't have space for a freezer.) But I love ice cream so dearly that I can't resist including this recipe for homemade ice cream in the cookbook. You'll love the thick creamy texture. This amount can be made nicely in a standard 4-quart or 5-quart hand-cranked or electric ice cream freezer.

1. First prepare the custard. Mix the milk and honey or maple syrup in the top part of a double boiler or in a medium-size pot. Heat until the mixture is warm and the honey is dissolved, stirring occasionally.
2. Beat the eggs in a separate bowl. Add a bit of the warm milk to the eggs, stir thoroughly, then stir back into the main bulk of the milk.
3. In the double boiler or straight over low heat, continue heating and stirring the mixture until it thickens into a thin custard. The mixture will coat a spoon dipped into it. Try to catch it before it begins to curdle, but if it does curdle a bit, don't worry. The custard will smooth out when you freeze it into ice cream.
4. Pour the custard into the inner metal container of the ice cream freezer and cool it thoroughly.
5. Mix in the cream and vanilla. The custard is now ready to freeze into ice cream. You can do it immediately or store it in the

refrigerator until you're ready.

6. To freeze the ice cream, put the inner metal container into the churn freezer assemble. Fill the outer bucket around the cylinder with layers of ice or snow and layers of regular salt or rock salt (about 2 cups salt total). Add enough cold water to make a thick slurry. Don't worry about exact measurements. Just get your mixture *cold*.

7. Making ice cream is most enjoyable if several people take turns churning. At first it will be easy, but as time goes on it gets harder and harder. As it gets harder, to get the smallest crystals and the smoothest ice cream, churn faster. When you suspect the ice cream is ready, open the top of the cylinder to check it. The ice cream should be quite thick, so don't give up until you have something really luscious.

8. Serve immediately , either just as it, or over any of the Cabbagetown desserts.

9. If you don't eat it all, store it in the freezer. Remove 15 minutes before serving so the ice cream can soften.

LEMON CINNAMON ICE CREAM

At step 5 mix in 1 teaspoon cinnamon and the grated rind of 1 lemon instead of the vanilla.

FRUIT ICE CREAM

Add 2 cups mashed fresh or frozen fruit to the ice cream just when it starts to get hard to crank. Continue churning until thick and rich. I especially love bananas, strawberries, and peaches.

Yield: 2 quarts. Serves 6–8

Metric Conversion Table

The cup and spoon measures used in this book are American, and thus slightly different from the British equivalents: An American cup contains 8 fluid ounces, and a British standard cup, 10; while an American tablespoon is roughly eqivalent to a British dessert spoon, and an American teaspoon 5/6 of a British Standard teaspoon.

AMERICAN	BRITISH	METRIC	IMPERIAL
1 teaspoon	5/6 teaspoon	5 ml.	1/6 fl. oz.
1 cup	1 dessert spoon	14.2 ml.	1/2 fl. oz.
1 cup	4/5 cup	227.2 ml.	8 fl.oz.

METRIC/IMPERIAL CONVERSION TABLE

1 lb.	=	454 grammes
4 oz.	=	100 grammes
1 pint	=	600 millilitres
1 quart	=	1 litre 200 ml.

Dawn scrubbing the back counter at the end of the night

INDEX